IN IT TO WIN IT

WINNING IN EVERY ROUND
VICTORIOUS CHRISTIAN LIVING

Kay,

May God's grace abound in your life.

Sincerely,

Pastor Earnestine Blakley

10-5-19

IN IT TO WIN IT

WINNING IN EVERY ROUND

Victorious Christian Living

PASTOR EARNESTINE BLAKLEY

INKWATER PRESS
PORTLAND • OREGON
INKWATERPRESS.COM

Scan QR Code to learn more about this title

Cover and interior design by Masha Shubin, Jayme Vincent
Edited by Andrew Durkin
Bible Closeup© wwwBillionPhotoscom. BigStockPhoto.com
© Photographer's Name. DreamsTime.com

Publisher: Inkwater Press | www.inkwaterpress.com

Paperback ISBN-13 978-1-62901-452-4 | ISBN-10 1-62901-452-4
Kindle ISBN-13 978-1-62901-453-1 | ISBN-10 1-62901-453-2

Printed in the U.S.A.

1 3 5 7 9 10 8 6 4 2

DEDICATION

I dedicate this book first and foremost to God because He is my Shepherd and I shall not want; to my loving husband, Charles, for his abundant support and encouragement; to our adult sons—Charles Jr. and Andrew—for their genuine way of nudging me along to fulfill my dream of writing this book; to the Ross Family, Blakley Family, and other family members who pray constantly for me that God's will and purpose be accomplished in my life; to the members of Hope Fellowship Church and H.O.P.E. Outreach Ministries, Inc., for their endless prayers and spiritual support to enable me to fulfill God's call in my life; and to everyone in my sphere of influence whom God has ordained to be an integral part of my life.

To all of you, I say, "Thank you!"

CONTENTS

Dedication......v

Introduction......ix

Chapter 1: Winning through Kingdom Living......1
God's Purpose Unfolds within Peter......5
Revelation from God......10
Building God's Kingdom......16
Secrets of the Kingdom......22
The Greatest in the Kingdom......26

Chapter 2: Winning through Confidence......33
Heavenly Reward......39
Heavenly Readiness......41
Heavenly Reassurance......43

Chapter 3: Winning through Matters of the Heart......47
A Heart of Forgiveness......49
Forgive Your Neighbor......52
A Heart of Love......55
Remove the Clutter......58

Chapter 4: Winning through Obedience....65
What's Love Got to Do with Obedience?....71
Led by the Holy Spirit....76
Obedience in the Valley....81

Chapter 5: Winning through the Cross....86
The Blood of Jesus Gives Atonement....88
The Blood of Jesus Gives Justification....89
The Blood of Jesus Gives Reconciliation....89
Evidence of the Cross....91
Change of Maliciousness....93
Change of Mindset....94
Change of Mission....95
Power to Rise Again....97

Chapter 6: Winning through God's Grace....105
Grace for the Fight....109
Grace When God Says "No"!....112
Assessment....115
Alignment....116
Acclaim....117

Chapter 7: Winning through Devotion to God....119
The Devotion of a Godly Mother....121
Qualities of a Godly Woman....124
Power to Live the Devoted Life....129
The Devoted Servant....134

Chapter 8: Winning through Freedom in Jesus....141
Three Ways to Be All That God Intended....145
The Bondage of Worry....147
Three Things That Worry Can Do....149
Saved from Sin's Shackles....151
Become a Christian....153

Bibliography....155

Meet the Author....157

INTRODUCTION

Over the course of my life, I can recall countless times when I felt overwhelmed, and somewhat defeated, by the relentless turmoil in my life. The constant reminder of the circumstances at hand gave me no relief. I prayed, but the problem remained staring me in the face. I rehearsed the circumstances in my mind, like a broken record played over and over again. There was a boxing match in my mind. I couldn't seem to escape the trouble. Have you ever been there? I'm sure you have experienced times when life's punches—such as financial problems, grief, relationship problems, health issues, and stress from life—spun you into a state of unrest.

As I waded through my mounds of issues, I asked myself, "Will I win this battle?" The Holy Spirit promptly assured me that the battle was His. Rather than being self-absorbed in my own problems and limited ability, God reminded me of His ability through me. I was suddenly reminded of the fact that God wants me to be victorious in every facet of my life. The Bible says in I Corinthians 15:57 (New International Version): "But thanks be to God! He gives us the victory through our Lord Jesus Christ."

I realized that my victory is in Jesus Christ. He made the ultimate blow to Satan when He died for us on the cross. The battle is already won! We have to remember to put on the whole armor of God, and we will be able to stand against the schemes of the devil. We can literally enjoy the victorious Christian living that God has promised in His Word. Ephesians 6:10–13 (NIV) says: "Finally, be strong in the Lord and in His mighty power. Put on the full armor of God so that you can take your stand against the devil's schemes. For our struggle is not against flesh and blood, but against the rulers, against the authorities, against the powers of this dark world, and against the spiritual forces of evil in the heavenly realms. Therefore put on the full armor of God, so that when the day of evil comes, you may be able to stand your ground, and after you have done everything, to stand."

The fact that God's word exhorts us to put on armor suggests that we are in a battle. We are in this battle to win and not to be defeated. We win by putting on the *spiritual* battle gear called "the full armor of God." This armor keeps us standing strong. The most notable victory is to remain standing when Satan sends us a blow from his force of deceivers. We have the power; we must remember to stand by the power of the Holy Spirit. The Bible says in Zechariah 4:6 (King James Version) that it is not by our own might or power, but it is by the Holy Spirit.

Ephesians 6:14–17 (NIV) says: "Stand firm, then, with the belt of truth buckled around your waist, with the breastplate of righteousness in place, and with your feet fitted with the readiness that comes from the Gospel of peace. In addition to all this, take up the shield of faith, with which you can extinguish all the flaming arrows of the evil one. Take the helmet of salvation and the sword of the Spirit, which is the word of God."

I put on the full armor of God daily during my prayer time, as though I was getting dressed. I put the armor on in order, starting with my head. I say, out loud, "I take on the helmet of salvation, the breastplate of righteousness, the belt of truth, the shoes of the Gospel of readiness, the sword of the Spirit which is the Word of God, and the shield of faith." I make Satan aware that I am dressed for battle, and I proceed forward in the confidence of the power of Jesus.

God's word is so explicit concerning spiritual warfare. He has given us the armor that will equip us to fight during these evil days. I am sure that there are times when you feel that you are fighting Satan one round after another in this wrestling match of life. In everyone's life, there are heavy-duty punches that seem to defeat us. No one is exempt from life's blows. Nevertheless, Jesus wants us to know that we are "in it to win it," and we can win in every round. The word "round" means one action or event in a series of actions or events. In every event, we can overcome the enemy. In Revelation 12:11 (KJV), we are told that we can overcome Satan by the blood of the Lamb and by the word of our testimony.

We have the power and authority to apply the blood of Jesus to our circumstances and declare the word of God in every action—in every round. The enemy, the devil has no choice but to flee. We have total victory over Satan. By being victorious over the enemy, we can excel in all areas of life. The word "victory" means success in winning or overcoming. Jesus has provided all that we need in order to overcome Satan's tactics. On a regular basis, I plead the blood of Jesus over difficult situations and over the life of my family members. For example, many times when praying over my boys, who both live in other cities, I say to God, "Lord, I plead the blood of Jesus over Charlie Jr. and Andrew, that you may protect them and keep them safe." I also plead the blood of Jesus over my husband, Charles Sr., as he teaches school or works with people on a daily basis. I realize that there is power in the blood of Jesus. "Pleading the blood of Jesus" means that we implore Jesus to defend us by applying His blood to a particular situation or specific people. These situations are actually like rounds in a boxing match or an athletic event. Every round we fight is in the hands of Jesus. In every round, we go higher in our relationship with the Lord.

The title of this book—*IN IT TO WIN IT: Winning in Every Round, Victorious Christian Living*—suggests that we need to imagine ourselves as victorious in all areas of our lives. I would like to encourage you to eradicate any negative thoughts from your mind, and any negative words from your vocabulary. Negative thoughts and words are contrary to God's ability to work on your behalf. God wants us, His children, to experience success in all of our undertakings. Yes, God has provided a way for us to win in life, and for us to overcome during painful trials and tribulations. We must remember to speak the word of God over our circumstances. Frequently I quote Isaiah 54:17 (New King James Version): "'No weapon formed against you shall prosper, and every tongue which rises against you in judgment you shall condemn. This is the heritage of the servants of the Lord, and their righteousness is from Me,' says the Lord."

We must speak God's Word and personalize it. Rather than saying "No weapon formed against you shall prosper," I say, "No weapon formed against *me* shall prosper." Before we can speak God's Word, we must believe what God is saying through it. If we don't believe God's Word personally, we won't take the time to speak it or apply it. It is easy to believe what God can do for someone else; but what about what God can do for you?

Therefore, as we begin this journey into victorious

Christian living, we must know that God wants His children to excel, and that He has provided the tools for each of us to overcome our troubles. This book provides tools and encouragement for all of us to reach the next level of spiritual growth. Many Christians become stagnant and fail to reach new heights in the Lord. Put on your spiritual boxing gloves as you read this book, and know that you are "in it to win it" as you live victoriously for Jesus, and that you are "winning in every round." Praise God!

CHAPTER ONE

WINNING THROUGH KINGDOM LIVING

But seek ye first the Kingdom of God, and His righteousness; and all these things shall be added unto you.

MATTHEW 6:33 (KJV)

Victory is attainable to everyone if the dwelling place is right. There is an internal dwelling place that gives us the propensity to achieve paramount success. God's will is for all of His children to accelerate beyond our wildest dreams. The dwelling place that I am referencing is the Kingdom of God. When I was a child, I dreamed of living in an enormous castle with plenty of rooms, wealth, and provisions. My dream has come true. That castle lives within me! Jesus is the King who has made it possible for all of God's children to make their abode in an everlasting kingdom. Since Jesus is my Good Shepherd, I have everything I need and want.

God's Kingdom is the dominion where God rules. God has a realm in which He governs our lives. I envision a throne in each of our hearts—one that is reserved exclusively for God, Jesus, and the Holy Spirit. Who is sitting on the throne in your heart? Whomever we allow to sit on the throne in our hearts is the person or thing that will master us. Jesus died so that God could occupy that special place in our hearts. Luke 17:21b (KJV) says that the Kingdom of God is within you. By taking this Scripture into consideration, kingdom authority dominates our lives if we have made Jesus Christ our Lord and Savior. We have no authority of our own. When we become a Christian, we relinquish all control to God.

In God's Kingdom, He rules in every area of our lives. Satan has no dominion. A seven-year old little girl, who loved Jesus, summarized this concept perfectly. She said, "Whenever the devil comes knocking on the door of my heart, I say, 'Jesus, could you please get the door?' Whenever the devil sees that it is Jesus who answered the door, he says, 'Sorry, I must have the wrong house,' and he leaves."

The above Christian approach to Satan seems simple, but it epitomizes how we need to respond when Satan attempts to gain access to our hearts. We must learn to give no place to the devil and his deceptive schemes. Jesus should be the keeper of the door to our hearts.

Jesus tells us in Matthew 6:10 (KJV) to ask for the Kingdom of God to come into our lives. This passage reads, "Thy kingdom come. Thy will be done, in earth, as it is in heaven." Jesus ushered in the Kingdom of God when He came to earth and died for our sins. Since He ascended into heaven, the same kingdom power that exists in heaven can exist here on earth. However, we must embrace the

Kingdom of God and welcome kingdom authority. We must pray that God's will be done in our lives. God's will is His purpose for us. Yes, we all were created for a purpose, and that purpose is inside all of us. Everything that is created has a purpose or reason for being in existence. I am reminded of a lead pencil, created by man but using God's wood. A lead pencil has everything inside to achieve its function—specifically, graphite, which is a soft carbon used as a writing material. Without being placed in the user's hand, the pencil is useless. Created by God, we are the same way. Without being surrendered to the Master's hand, we are useless. We have everything inside us to fulfill God's purpose. God has placed special gifts and abilities inside of His children; these were intended to edify the body of Christ and win the lost to His Kingdom. Therefore, we must leave our comfort zones and surrender to the hand of God so that we can do what He has called us to do.

We all have a centralized purpose in that we are to win lost souls to Jesus Christ. We advance the Kingdom of God by inviting souls to give their hearts to Jesus. God created us for that purpose. Ephesians 2:10 (KJV) says, "For we are His workmanship, created in Christ Jesus unto good works, which God hath before ordained that we should walk in them."

Hooray! We can stop laboring over our purpose in life. God has defined it so clearly by saying that we are created to do good works. As we do the good works, our purpose will unfold. Purpose unfolds as we serve God and serve others. Not only does purpose unfold, it is also progressive. Every experience builds upon another in order to formulate God's perfect plan for our lives. We are not all that God has created us to be in one season of life. Each season builds upon the next. Many times we feel as though we should be doing something great. Obeying God day by day and step by step is great in His eyes because we are doing the good works that He ordained for us before the foundation of the world.

Mother Theresa once said, "We can do no great things, only small things with great love." Our goal in life should be to do little acts of kindness, and the rewards will be immeasurable. Our purpose is determined by doing God's will in every dimension of our lives. It is not just one big act and we are finished. Purpose unfolds daily, and it is progressive.

When I was an adolescent, one of my primary chores was to work on our cotton farm in the Missouri Bootheel—in a small town called Steele, Missouri. As I worked in the blazing sun for at least ten hours a day, I often wondered what my purpose was in life. I had dreams of going to college and becoming a school teacher. "But what about right now?" I thought. "Will my dream of becoming a teacher become a reality?"

I learned early in life that we have to wait on our dreams. God's purpose for that moment was for me to work on the cotton farm and help my family bring in a harvest. There were fourteen children in the Ross family, and I am second in birth order. All of us, including my parents—Thomas Bob and Mary Anna Ross—worked hard to have a productive crop. Every year our labor was not in vain. Sure, some years were more productive than others; nevertheless, God always provided. By working on the cotton farm, I learned the value of hard work and perseverance. Nothing is wasted with God; He uses all of our experiences for His purpose and glory. All fourteen of us fulfilled our dreams in one form or another; all of us have grown up to be hard workers and servants of our Lord and Savior Jesus Christ.

God revealed to me recently that just as I had worked hard on the farm to bring about a harvest of cotton, today I am bringing about a harvest of souls. Purpose was being achieved then—and purpose is being achieved today, as I preach and teach God's Word to thousands, including those who listen to my radio broadcast and watch my television program in St. Joseph, Missouri, and surrounding states and cities.

As we contemplate our purpose, remember the words that God spoke in Jeremiah 29:11 (KJV): "For I know the thoughts that I think toward you, saith the Lord, thoughts of peace, and not of evil, to give you an expected end." We can see that God does not want any of us to fail. He wants us to win in every area of our lives. God knew His plans for us before the foundation of the world, and He desires to help us prosper, giving us great success in all of our undertakings. It is reassuring to know that God thought about us before the world began. All of His thoughts are for our good and not for evil.

GOD'S PURPOSE UNFOLDS WITHIN PETER

As I studied portions of Matthew, Chapter 16 (NIV), I began to observe how God's purpose was unfolding for Peter. I noticed that Peter had good experiences and bad experiences. But the bad experiences did not devalue God's purpose for him. I would like to examine three aspects of Peter's trajectory of purpose with Jesus.

1. Peter confessed.

In this segment, we will notice that Peter actually confessed who Jesus was to His face. Part of knowing our purpose is to know who Jesus is for us personally. The word "confess" means to admit as true or to acknowledge as true. Peter, under the guidance of the Holy Spirit, certainly achieved this objective by giving an accurate statement about who

Jesus is. Matthew 16:13–14 (NIV) says: When Jesus came to the region of Caesarea Philippi, He asked His disciples, "Who do people say the Son of Man is?" They replied, "Some say John the Baptist; others say Elijah; and still others, Jeremiah or one of the prophets."

By asking this question, Jesus could assess how the other disciples were thinking about Him. Jesus was traveling through Caesarea Philippi, a region that was extremely pagan. He thought that this would be a good time to find out just what was in His disciples' hearts. Although Jesus is all-knowing, he wanted to hear it verbalized.

In Matthew 16:15 (NIV), Jesus asks, "But what about you? Who do you say I am?"

Of course Peter answered first. In Matthew 16:16 (NIV) Simon Peter answered, "You are the Christ, the Son of the living God." This was an accurate confession. Peter had truly given an accurate answer to Jesus. Peter knew that Jesus was the Christ, which means the anointed one. Jesus Christ is the true Son of the living God.

2. Peter was commended.

In this aspect of Peter's experience of purpose, we see that Jesus commends Peter. The word "commend" means to praise or to bless. Jesus was definitely pleased with Peter's response because it was prompted by the Holy Spirit. Jesus says in Matthew 16:17–18 (NIV), "Blessed are you, Simon son of Jonah, for this was not revealed to you by man, but by My Father in heaven. And I tell you that you are Peter, and on this rock I will build My church, and the gates of Hades will not overcome it."

Jesus defined purpose within Peter by saying "You are Peter." In another passage of Scripture, Jesus told Peter that he would be called "Cephas," which means a stone. The word "Peter" comes from the Greek word *Petros,* which means detached stone. The church was not built upon Peter because Peter means an individual stone. The church is built upon the rock—the word in the Greek is *petra*—a very large solid rock. The church is built on the revealed knowledge that Jesus is the Christ, the Son of the living God. Jesus is the true foundation upon which the church is built. The Bible says in I Peter 2:7 (KJV) that the stone the builders disallowed has become the head of the corner or the chief cornerstone. Although Jesus was rejected and persecuted, He is now the head of the church. All the demonic forces in hell and the dark world cannot stand against His church.

Jesus continued to commend Peter by giving him the keys of the kingdom. In Matthew 16:19 (NIV), he says, "I will give you the keys of the Kingdom of Heaven; whatever you bind on earth will be bound in heaven, and whatever you loose on earth will be loosed in heaven." This is a powerful promise from Jesus to us that we can bind and loose with our words. The word "keys" here means the authority to announce. We have the authority to announce that strongholds can be bound and that blessings and peace can be loosed. Whatever we bind on earth will be bound in heaven, and whatever we loose on earth will be loosed in heaven. Our words have power. We have access and entry into heaven with the keys of binding and loosing.

3. Peter was corrected.

A final aspect of Peter's purpose in this passage of Matthew Chapter 16 (NIV) is the fact that Jesus had to correct Peter. It is amazing that Peter confessed Jesus as the Christ and was commended by Jesus, and then so quickly he was corrected by Jesus. One meaning of the word "correct" is to scold or rebuke. Jesus had to rebuke Peter because he was allowing Satan to use him. Matthew 16:21 (NIV) says, "From that time on, Jesus began to explain to His disciples that He must go to Jerusalem and suffer many things at the hands of the elders, chief priests, and teachers of the law, and that He must be killed and on the third day be raised to life."

Jesus was trying to explain to His disciples His purpose for coming to earth. He wanted to prepare them for the things that He would suffer. Nevertheless, Peter would not have any part of this bad news. Therefore, he rebuked Jesus. Matthew 16:22 (NIV) says, Peter took Him aside and began to rebuke Him. "Never, Lord!" he said. "This shall never happen to you!"

Peter was trying to protect Jesus; but he did not know the Scriptures. He was moving in the flesh and not in the Spirit. Jesus rebuked him by scolding him sharply. Matthew 16:23 (NIV) says, Jesus turned and said to Peter, "Get behind Me, Satan! You are a stumbling block to Me; you do not have in mind the things of God, but the things of men."

Peter was very human in achieving the purpose of God. Jesus had blessed and praised him earlier, and then he was reprimanded. Every one of us is a work in progress. Just because we make mistakes does not mean that our purpose is nullified. Poor character or bad choices do not devalue our purpose. Peter is still "Cephas," which means stone. Peter later became one of the pillars of the church. God used him mightily. However, he did not always do or say the right things. We all make mistakes. We should grow from our mistakes and continue to climb higher in our purpose for the Kingdom of God.

We must remember that the word "purpose" refers to God's will for our lives. It is important to know what God's purpose is in every season of our lives. I heard a friend tell this story about a husband and wife who went out of business. They put a sign on the door of their establishment that read as follows: "Gone out of business. Didn't know what our business was."

If we don't know what our business is for the Lord, then we will fail. Knowing our purpose gives us a sense of direction. As we progress in our purpose to walk in the Kingdom of God, we must know what God's will is for us at that moment. God's will always involves winning lost souls for the kingdom, and doing good works. God's will always involves glorifying God. Knowledge of God's will navigates us down the right path. We don't have to understand everything, but it is crucial that we obey God's voice step by step. The Holy Spirit will not let us fall. We all have a sphere of influence that encompasses the people we are to impact, whether it is at home, work, school, church, or elsewhere in our community. God's will or purpose is unleashed as we perform good deeds in that particular realm. Romans 14:17 (New Living Translation) says that the Kingdom of God is not a matter of what we eat or drink, but of living a life of goodness and peace and joy in the Holy Spirit. As we live our lives for Jesus, goodness, peace, and joy will unfold.

The Kingdom of God is the realm in which God rules. As we allow God to rule and reign in our hearts, we will discover that God will take us to new levels. Our minds can't even imagine all the good things that God has in store for us. As the Bible tells us in I Corinthians 2:9 (KJV), "But as it is written, Eye hath not seen, nor ear heard, neither have entered into the heart of man, the things which God hath prepared for them that love Him." The things that God has in store for us are so unimaginable that we cannot fathom the next level of blessings in our lives.

You might ask, "What do I do when I am not succeeding and my life seems unproductive?" Many people feel as though they are stuck in a rut, or that they are overcome by life's challenges. The Kingdom of God has a solution for that dilemma. Jesus tells us not to worry when we are in a state of lack or need. The important thing is to continue seeking His Kingdom. Jesus says in Matthew 6:33–34 (NIV), "But seek first His Kingdom and His righteousness, and all these things will be given to you as well. Therefore do not worry about tomorrow, for tomorrow will worry about itself. Each day has enough trouble of its own."

REVELATION FROM GOD

Kingdom living involves revelation from God. The word "revelation" means to make known or to disclose. Since the Kingdom of God is the realm or dominion in which God rules, we must get a glimpse of what He has in store for us. What did God have in mind for us before the creation of the world? I believe as we unravel God's purpose for our lives, we must internalize the scope of His plans for putting us on this earth in the first place. Little by little, God discloses those mysteries to us.

Psalm 37:4 (KJV) says, "Delight thyself also in the Lord; and He shall give thee the desires of thine heart." Those ideas that materialize in our minds regarding our career and our vocation did not just pop into existence out of the cosmos. When we truly delight ourselves in the Lord, He will drop ideas into our minds and hearts. Those insights become our passion, and we begin to gravitate toward those yearnings. We might even ask ourselves, "I am really considering becoming a nurse. Where did that idea come from?

God will put desires in us that He has already planned for us to achieve. There is a lady in our church who has three children. For years she was concerned with just making a living, not with making a life. As a single mother, she worked at whatever establishment would employ her. She lived from paycheck to paycheck, barely making ends meet. Intuitively, she began to feel a desire to become a nurse. The more she served the Lord, the stronger that yearning became. God literally opened doors for her to get her education free of charge due to her circumstances, and she is now enrolled in the nursing program at a local university to get her RN Degree in Nursing. I always say, "Where God guides, He provides."

God reveals to us what He already sees. In His dealings with us, He begins with the end in mind. Ephesians 1:4 (NLT) says: "Even before He made the world, God loved us and chose us in Christ to be holy and without fault in His eyes." It is evident that God saw in advance that we are to be like Him. God is holy and He wants His children to be holy, which means to be set apart. Whatever our course of action might be, God wants us to exemplify a holy lifestyle and to live in a manner pleasing to Him. We must remember that we were created for good works that God planned in advance for us to do (Ephesians 2:10, KJV).

God begins with the end in mind. Even when you were in your mother's womb, God knew what you would become. David says in Psalm 139:15–16 (NIV), "My frame was not hidden from you when I was made in the secret place. When I was woven together in the depths of the earth, Your eyes saw my unformed body. All the days ordained for me were written in Your book before one of them came to be."

In the above passage, the book referred to is God's heavenly register, where He records all of His decisions about us. He even records every tear that we shed, and He collects our tears in a bottle (Psalm 56:8, KJV). God truly loves us, and all of His plans for us are good. David states that even when he was in his mother's womb, God saw his unformed body. We have always been on God's mind. He knows our end from the beginning.

Isaiah 46:10 (KJV) states: "Declaring the end from the beginning, and from ancient times the things that are not yet done, saying, My counsel shall stand, and I will do all my pleasure." God does not change His mind about us; His purpose is settled. One friend of mine said that it seems as if God has circled on a map what His plans are for us, and that those plans will come to fruition. Whatever God circles on His map will happen. Nevertheless, we must learn to wait for God's appointed time. The best kind of faith is "waiting faith." Delays are not denials. We must learn to wait upon the Lord.

Habakkuk 2:3 (NIV) says: "For the revelation awaits an appointed time; it speaks of the end and will not prove false. Though it linger, wait for it; it will certainly come and will not delay." If we do not have the ability to wait, we will miss God's appointed time. God sees the whole picture, and He is working out every detail. He is orchestrating events, people, and places so that every facet will coincide with His perfect plan.

The story is told about two bricklayers. A young girl, around eight years old, was passing by a church construction site. She asked one bricklayer, "Hey, Mister. What you doing?"

"Can't you see that I am laying bricks?" he replied.

Persistently, she went to the next bricklayer and asked the same question. "Hey, Mister," she said. "What you doing?"

He responded in a positive manner: "Little girl, I am building a cathedral."

Do you see the difference in the responses? One bricklayer was only laying bricks while the other one was building a cathedral. The latter bricklayer saw the whole picture—the finished product. That is the way God looks at us. He sees the end from the beginning. He knows the finished product of what he is accomplishing in each of us.

There is a lady by the name of Anna. Her story is told in Luke 2:36–38 (KJV). As I read Anna's story, I understood that the hand of God was truly upon her. Anna broke down every barrier one might think of, and she impacted the Kingdom of God. Anna was filled with the Holy Spirit. She possessed the gift of prophecy, which meant that she would *foretell* and *forth-tell* God's word. "Foretell" means that she would speak what was going to happen before it happened. "Forth-tell" means that Anna would speak forth what God told her to say. "Anna" means "grace." Her father's name was Phanuel, which means "The face or appearance of God." Just by observing the names that were given to Anna and her father, one could tell that God's hand was upon that family. Remember, God knows the end from the beginning.

Anna was one of the first to see the baby Jesus in the temple. She was from the tribe of Asher—one of Jacob's twelve sons who became the "Twelve Tribes of Israel." In Genesis 49:20 (NIV), a prophecy was spoken over Asher by his father Jacob, more than three millennia ago. It stated the following: *Asher's food will be rich; he will provide delicacies fit for a king.* I believe when Anna offered praises and thanksgiving to the baby Jesus in the temple, she provided the delicacies fit for King Jesus. This was a blessed opportunity that she had waited years to witness. Anna waited in the temple for the coming of Jesus. Anna's life was prophesied as early as 1400 years before she was born.

Luke 2:36b–37 (NIV) says: "She was very old; she had lived with her husband seven years after her marriage, and then was a widow until she was eighty-four. She never left the temple but worshiped night and day, fasting and praying." Anna was a devout woman. She stayed in the temple day and night, worshiping her God. Despite her age, she accomplished something only Simeon had accomplished, and that was to meet and give thanks for the Christ

Child. Before Simeon died, he saw the Christ Child just as God had promised him he would (Luke 2:25–26, KJV).

Anna broke down three major barriers. She was old—around 105 years old, according to the Bible; she was a widow, so she was probably poor and lacked social status; and she was a woman—women were second-class citizens in those days. However, look at what Anna accomplished! She came up to Mary, Joseph, and Jesus right after Simeon had blessed Jesus. She was the aged widow woman who graced Jesus with her words and presence. She was able to address the entire crowd assembled there, and told them that Jesus was the one who was prophesied as the Messiah or the Christ, which means "Anointed One." She shared with the crowd that Jesus was their redeemer or deliverer. Everyone was ministered to by her words. The barriers did not deter Anna. She accomplished great things for her Lord.

Luke 2:40 (KJV) says that the Christ Child grew and became strong; He was filled with wisdom, and the grace of God was upon Him. I believe that Anna's influence impacted Jesus's life. She praised God for Him and she prayed day and night for Him.

Anna is an example of a person who was in this Christian race to win it, and she was determined to win in every round or season of her life. As Christians, we must not underestimate our value to the Kingdom of God. Despite the obstacles or barriers, we are more than conquerors. Romans 8:37 (NIV) says, "No, in all these things we are more than conquerors through Him who loved us." Just like Anna, we must be consecrated and devout in our service to the Kingdom of God. I know we cannot stay in the temple or church day and night. But the temple of God is on the inside of us. God reveals to us his plans for us and nothing can stop us except our failure to respond to the promptings of God. Without getting a revelation of who we are, we will never become the people we were created to become.

I am reminded of a story that I heard years ago. There was an eagle's egg that got mixed in with some chicken eggs that were in the process of being hatched. After the eggs were hatched, the young eaglet thought it was a chicken. It clucked around the farmyard; it pecked in the dirt like the other chickens. Things couldn't have been better for the eaglet. Then one day, it saw this majestic bird with a huge wingspan soaring in the sky. It was fantastic! The eaglet asked the other chickens, "What is that?" One hen who was nearby replied, "Oh, that's an eagle. You will never be like him. He has huge talons, large wings, keen vision, and can fly higher than any other bird. So just forget about it."

With a huge sigh, the eaglet was disappointed to be told that it could never become like the bird that it had witnessed in the sky. However, the eaglet could not forget the image that had been formulated in its mind on that bright summer day. Somehow, it had connected with the eagle that was in the sky. There was an instant identification. Passion was stirred inside the eaglet to become just like that bird it had witnessed high in the sky.

Years passed and the eaglet became an adult bird with an abiding yearning to fly higher than the chickens in the farmyard. Instinctively, it flapped its wings and began to fly higher and higher. Finally, it was soaring just like the large bird it had seen in the sky on that unforgettable day. As the eagle soared higher, it realized that its purpose was to soar and not peck around on the ground with the chickens.

What about you? Have you seen the image of yourself that God has for you? You too were not created to peck around with people who have no goals or vision. People who have no revelation from God about their purpose will want to keep you on their level. We must rise up and soar and become all that God has created us to become! Get into the Word of God daily and pray without ceasing; God will reveal to you His purpose. Remember, purpose is a journey—not a one-time destination. We achieve purpose progressively with God as the navigator. God has beautiful plans for all of His children. "Where there is no vision, the people perish," as stated in Proverbs 29:18 (KJV).

BUILDING GOD'S KINGDOM

As Christians, we are building God's Kingdom by building our own lives for His glory. We must envision ourselves as God's building. Before anyone begins a building project, he or she must gather the materials. God provides quality spiritual materials for us to construct His building. We are that building! The Bible says in Ephesians 2:22 (NIV): "And in Him you too are being built together to become a dwelling in which God lives by His Spirit." God builds us up as we surrender ourselves to His mighty hands. Our part in the building process is to become yielded vessels that God can use; we must be a construction site that God can build up as He chooses. As we win lost souls to the Kingdom of God, we help to multiply it for all eternity.

The Lord must build our spiritual house or our labor is in vain. There is nothing worse than to build a structure and have to tear it down again. We waste time and money when we are foolish builders. We should choose to allow God to build us, using His materials. Of course, we do have a choice. So many times we choose the world's building materials out of necessity or convenience. Needless to say, the results are always disastrous. Counterfeit materials will never replace the supernatural materials that God has designed just for His children. God's plans are for us to come to the Living Stone who is Jesus, and allow ourselves as living stones to be built on His foundation. I Peter 2:4–5 (New King James Version) says: "Coming to Him as to a living stone, rejected indeed by men, but chosen by God and precious, you also, as living stones, are being built up a spiritual house, a holy priesthood, to offer up spiritual sacrifices acceptable to God through Jesus Christ."

Whenever I read this passage of Scripture, I am reminded of the story of the Three Little Pigs. If you are familiar with this classic children's story, you will recall that one little pig built a house of straw, and the next built a house of sticks. Only the third little pig built a house of bricks, which withstood all attempts to attack the house. As spiritual houses for God, when we build our houses using spiritual materials, we will survive turmoil and distress. We will not succumb to the destructive forces of the devil.

It is reassuring to realize that we are a holy priesthood, which means that we are set apart unto God and that we can go straight to the throne room of heaven. We do not need a priest to go before God for us because we ourselves are priests; we are a royal priesthood according to I Peter 2:9 (NIV). We go through Jesus to get to the Father. When we humbly surrender ourselves to God as a living sacrifice through Jesus Christ, He accepts our offering. It is pleasing to Him because we have come before Him with a yielded heart; we can offer sacrifices of praise and thanksgiving and God will accept them favorably.

We are works in progress. Day by day, God is building us into a spiritual house. As He builds, he chips away the undesirable traits that tend to surface during our daily living. We are being conformed into the image of Jesus Christ. Our house must look like Jesus. I read a story about a sculptor who had sculpted a magnificent lion out of stone. Everyone marveled over this lion. The one question that was asked constantly was, "How did you construct such a magnificent lion?" His reply was, "That's simple. I chipped away everything that did not look like a lion."

Our heavenly Creator, God, is chipping away everything about us that does not look like Jesus Christ. Our spiritual house must look like Jesus' spiritual house. Others will notice our magnificence and will want to follow Jesus. All that we become is because of the hand of God by His Spirit.

There are three ways that we can build God's Kingdom. Each of these biblical principles will enable us to be wise builders of God's Kingdom. The first way that we can build God's Kingdom is to *hear the word of God.* Jesus says in Matthew 7:24 (NIV): "Therefore everyone who hears these words of mine and puts them into practice is like a wise man who built his house on the rock." We must hear the word of God and put it into practice. It can be relatively easy to hear the word and proceed with your daily routine. The true test of being wise is when we put God's word into practice. A wise builder builds upon the rock, something solid. Of course, we know that the rock is Jesus Christ. God does not want us to be shaky and flaky Christians. Strong materials from heaven will allow us to construct a strong spiritual house.

Jesus continues to say in Matthew 7:25 (NIV): "The rain came down, the streams rose, and the winds blew and beat against that house, yet it did not fall, because it had its foundation on the rock." We need not only a strong house, but a solid foundation—one that is built on Jesus, the solid rock. Trials are going to come, and they will test the soundness of our structure. What shakes us up will not shake us apart when we have our foundation on the rock. When we get the word of God inside us and put God's word into practice, we will be strong. But if we hear God's words and do not put them into practice, we will have a great fall.

Jesus tells us in Matthew 7:26–27 (NIV): "But everyone who hears these words of mine and does not put them into practice is like a foolish man who built his house on sand. The rain came down, the streams rose, and the winds blew and beat against that house, and it fell with a great crash."

What kind of builder are you? Are you a wise or a foolish builder? The wise builder hears the word of God and puts it into practice, whereas the foolish builder hears the word and does not put it into practice. Do you take pride in going to church and hearing God's Word, and then forget what it says? Perhaps your objective for hearing God's Word is to impress someone else. The true test is to put God's Word into practice. In the Book of James 1:22 (NKJV), we are told: "But be doers of the Word, and not hearers only, deceiving yourselves."

I have a quote that I heard many years ago and that I share with others: "It is not how much Bible you can quote but how much Bible you can tote." This statement tells us that quoting Scripture alone is not the total picture. Our words can be heartless. God wants us to put the Word into practice by carrying it in our hearts and living by it. The word "tote" denotes that we are able to carry the Word of God in our hearts and apply it.

A second way to build God's Kingdom is to *build on the foundation of Jesus.* A foundation is a base on which a structure rests. In Isaiah 28:16 (NIV), Isaiah made a prophecy around 700 BC that says: So this is what the Sovereign Lord says: "See, I lay a stone in Zion, a tested stone, a precious cornerstone for a sure foundation; the one who trusts will never be dismayed." Jesus is the real foundation; one does not have to worry about sinking or falling apart. He was tested when He suffered and died for us on the cross. We will not be disappointed when we put our trust in Him.

The apostle Paul said in I Corinthians 3:10–11 (NIV):

"By the grace God has given me, I laid a foundation as an expert builder, and someone else is building on it. But each one should be careful how he builds. For no one can lay any foundation other than the one already laid, which is Jesus Christ." The apostle Paul spread the true Gospel of Jesus Christ. He was an expert builder because He was directly led by the Holy Spirit in everything he said or did. When the apostle Paul said that someone was building on the foundation that he laid, he was talking about Apollos, a fellow servant of Jesus Christ. We are building on it too when we spread the Good News of Jesus Christ. There is no other foundation than the one that has already been laid. Ephesians 2:19–20 (NIV) says: "Consequently, you are no longer foreigners and strangers, but fellow citizens with God's people and also members of His household, built on the foundation of the apostles and prophets, with Christ Jesus Himself as the Chief Cornerstone." All of the apostles and prophets laid a foundation when they preached Jesus Christ and the entire Gospel message. We all must be careful that we are not deceived into thinking that there is a new Gospel or new message from Jesus that has not been stated in the Bible. Jesus is the Chief Cornerstone. Everything must build upon Him. There are no updates of the Bible because the truth does not need to be updated!

A third way to build God's Kingdom is to *build others up.* Proverbs 11:30 (NKJV) says: "And he who wins souls is wise." The greatest miracle is salvation. The only thing we can take to heaven with us is another soul. Many times when I officiate at funerals, I see people putting material things in the coffin with the deceased. I know they do this for comfort, but those items do not make it into heaven. The only thing that goes to heaven is that person's born-again soul, which has already departed from the body. At that point, the body is an empty shell. True wisdom is expressed by winning souls to the Kingdom of God. We build others up spiritually when we tell them the Gospel message and give them an opportunity to respond by inviting Jesus into their hearts. If Jesus is not in our hearts when we die, Hell will be our eternal home.

I Thessalonians 5:11 (NIV) says: "Therefore encourage one another and build each other up, just as in fact you are doing." Are you a good encourager? My mother, Mary Anna Ross, is an excellent encourager. At the age of eighty-four, she still tells people everywhere she goes about Jesus, and that everything is going to be alright. She begins her conversations by saying, "Isn't God good?" With that leading question, people will either receive her and continue to talk, or reject her and walk away. However, she is willing to take the risk. The rejections are worth it if she can find one person that she can encourage during her excursions.

Ephesians 4:29 (NIV) says: "Do not let any unwholesome talk come out of your mouths, but only what is helpful for building others up according to their needs, that it may benefit those who listen." People are listening to what we are saying. We must make sure that our words are fruitful and nourishing, words that will build others up and not tear them down. The words that we speak have power; they can build others up or tear them down. I always say that hurtful words are like squeezing toothpaste from a tube. Once you squeeze it out, you cannot put it back inside.

In building God's Kingdom, we are being conformed to the image of Jesus Christ. We must yield our members to the hand of God everyday so that He can shape and mold us. This shaping takes time and discipline. We are works in progress.

I remember a story I heard once that tells of a lady who was tremendously overweight. She enrolled herself in a weight-loss clinic and was put under the care of a supervisor.

The supervisor drew a silhouette on a mirror, representing the shape the lady wished to become. The supervisor told her that her goal was to fit into the shape that was in the mirror. When the lady first looked in the mirror, her body extended significantly outside of the silhouette. She felt a sense of discouragement. But she regained her focus and disciplined herself by eating right and exercising regularly. After a few weeks, she looked in the mirror again. Her body still extended outside the silhouette, but not as much as before. After several months, she looked in the mirror again, and to her amazement she fit perfectly inside the silhouette. Her body had conformed to the image in the mirror. She did not lose the weight overnight. It took time, discipline, and a healthy lifestyle. The same is true with us spiritually. We are not conformed into the image of Jesus Christ overnight. It takes time, discipline, and a spiritual lifestyle. We must stay focused and allow the hand of God to shape us into a spiritual house.

SECRETS OF THE KINGDOM

As we consider winning through Kingdom living, we have to learn the secrets of the Kingdom. A secret is hidden knowledge or a lack of revelation. One way these secrets are revealed to believers is through parables. A parable is an earthly story with a heavenly meaning. Jesus used parables so that some would be permitted to understand the secrets of the Kingdom and some would not.

Why did Jesus permit His disciples to understand the secrets of the Kingdom of God, while denying that understanding to others? We only tell secrets to people we trust, or people in our sphere of influence. We don't tell secrets to our enemies. Jesus was attempting to avoid a premature death; therefore, He did not want His opposition knowing deep things about the Kingdom. Jesus said in Matthew 13:12 (NIV), "Whoever has will be given more, and he will have an abundance. Whoever does not have, even what he has will be taken from him." Those of us who are Christians will be given an abundance of revelation from our Lord because of our love for Him and His love for us. But the enemy will lose whatever understanding he has about the Kingdom.

A parable teaches a vital lesson, mostly dealing with nature or human life. Jesus explains why He speaks in parables in Matthew 13:13–14 (NIV): "This is why I speak to them in parables: Though seeing, they do not see; though hearing, they do not hear or understand. But blessed are your eyes because they see, and your ears because they hear." The enemies of Jesus hear His parables and they take what he is saying literally; they fail to see or understand the deeper meaning. As believers, we are able to hear and understand the parables because of revelatory knowledge from heaven; as a result, we are blessed by the truths that we have received and internalized in our hearts.

In the parable of the sower, which is found in Matthew 13:18–23 (KJV), Jesus talks about four kinds of soil (a metaphor for the human heart), and the seeds that are sown in each. The first kind of soil is found along the path. The seed is the Word of God or the Gospel message. We are sowers of the seeds. The Word that is sown along the path is snatched away by the devil before it is understood. Since the path is hard, the seed lies on top of the ground and does not have time to become internalized. The objective of Satan is to steal every seed that is planted in our hearts. Therefore, we must cultivate the soil of our hearts so that the seed can take root and grow into a mighty harvest.

The second kind of soil is the rocky soil, filled with rocks that choke the plant. Because of the massive amount of rocks, the plant cannot take root and grow. The person with hard places in their heart receives the Word with joy, but quickly falls away. The word cannot take root. Therefore, there is no fruit. We must be rooted and grounded in the Word of God. If not, when the first sign of trouble occurs, we will quickly fall away from our walk with the Lord.

I was talking to a man today, and he told me that sin prevented the Word from taking root in his life. He had sinful habits that he allowed to dominate his life. His sinful lifestyle created rocks in his heart that prevented him from being productive. He stopped coming to church, and he stopped serving the ministries in which he was once involved. Currently, he is taking strides to remove those rocks of sin with the aid of the Holy Spirit. He has repented of his sinful behavior and is focused on Jesus in his renewed walk. He is attending church on a regular basis again, and is serving in the ministries that he once served. This young man had to first allow the Holy Spirit to remove the hardness from his heart. This occurred when he repented of his sins.

A third kind of soil is the thorny soil. People with thorns in their hearts have a great deal of pain or worries. These worries can cause distractions, thus making their lives unfruitful. We can become so engrossed with the cares of life that the Word of God gets choked out of our lives. In times of pain and trouble, we need to seek God and His Kingdom and everything that we need will be provided for us.

The fourth kind of soil is the good soil. A heart that is characterized as good soil is the heart that hears and receives the Word of God. Readiness is the key to understanding God's Word. When we understand the Word, we internalize it and become doers of it. The good soil is our goal as Christians.

I heard a story about a man in England who loved

flowers. As a result of his love, he carried flower seeds in his pockets and scattered them wherever he went. Over a period of time, there were beautiful flowers all along the countryside for people to enjoy. However, he noticed that there were certain parts of England where he had scattered an abundance of seeds, but they did not produce. He quickly realized that the soil there was not suitable for growth. It was either on the path, or it was rocky, or it was thorny. Only the good soil produced an abundance of gorgeous flowers.

Jesus told His disciples another parable—this time about weeds. A weed is an undesirable plant. In Matthew 13:24–27 (NIV), Jesus told His disciples the following: "The Kingdom of Heaven is like a man who sowed good seed in his field. But while everyone was sleeping, his enemy came and sowed weeds among the wheat, and went away. When the wheat sprouted and formed heads, then the weeds also appeared. The owner's servants came to him and said, 'Sir, didn't you sow good seed in your field? Where then did the weeds come from?'"

If you have ever planted anything, you know how annoying weeds can be. They can grow up overnight and stand so tall above the actual plants. Weeds can actually become so intertwined with the rooting system of the good plant that it will become detrimental to remove them. In Matthew 13:28–30 (NIV), Jesus explains what is happening in the parable when he says that "an enemy did this." The servants asked him if he wanted them to pull up the weeds. "No," he answered, "because while you are pulling the weeds, you may root up the wheat with them. Let both grow together until the harvest. At that time I will tell the harvesters: First collect the weeds and tie them in bundles to be burned; then gather the wheat and bring it into my barn."

The disciples did not understand what Jesus was saying

in this parable. After the crowd had left, they asked Jesus to explain it. Jesus answered in Matthew 13:37–41: "The one who sowed the good seed is the Son of Man. The field is the world, and the good seed stands for the sons of the kingdom. The weeds are the sons of the evil one. And the enemy who sows them is the devil. The harvest is the end of the age, and the harvesters are angels. As the weeds are pulled up and burned in the fire, so it will be at the end of the age. The Son of Man will send out His angels, and they will weed out of His Kingdom everything that causes sin and all who do evil."

We as Christians are good seeds that Jesus has planted in the field, the world. We are in this world, but not of it. The devil and false Christians try to distract us and uproot our faith. Judgment Day will come when the devil and his angels will be cast into a fiery furnace, and there will be weeping and gnashing of teeth.

Matthew 13:43 (KJV) tells us that the righteous will shine like the sun in the kingdom of their Father, and he who has ears, let him hear. We will live and reign with Jesus forever in the Kingdom of Heaven. Our brightness will be like the sun, shinning into all eternity. Jesus wants us to hear and understand this spiritual truth. The devil might appear to be winning in your life, but we will this war. The end of the age is near, and we are in this race to win it.

THE GREATEST IN THE KINGDOM

Greatness is defined as being important or being the best. In the natural realm, everyone strives to excel and do their best in life's undertakings. Our natural paradigm is to acquire positions of high status or to reach for the stars. But what about greatness in the Kingdom of God? Should we seek to be the best in the Kingdom? Greatness in the Kingdom is prefaced on "condition" and not "position." God looks at the *condition* of our hearts to see if we are surrendered to His will; He is not concerned about what *position* we hold on special boards or councils, although God can open doors for those blessings. Neither is God concerned about us seeking *positions* of greatness in His Kingdom. Kingdom aspirations are centered on making God number one and acknowledging Him as our source of everything. When this happens, we will be willing to serve God and others. Greatness is measured by how well we serve. Matthew 23:11 (KJV) says that the greatest among you shall be your servant. As Christians, we must realize that God works through us, and that all that we achieve is due to His power. God is pleased when He can get the ultimate glory, because we allow our bodies to be conduits of His power as we serve others.

David said it best in his prayer of praise in I Chronicles 29:11 (NLT): "Yours, O Lord, is the greatness, the power, the glory, the victory, the majesty. Everything in the heavens and on earth is yours, O Lord, and this is Your Kingdom. We adore you as the One who is over all things."

When we truly acknowledge that all power comes from God, we will yearn to have his power operating in our lives. If anything significant happens to us, we will be ready to give God the glory. An ax, for instance, cannot boast about the amount of wood that it cuts down in a given day. The credit goes to the woodcutter. The axe is only a tool in the woodcutter's hand. The same is true with us as Christians. We cannot boast about how many souls we lead to the Lord or how much money we make. We are a tool in God's hand. The glory goes to God. It is His ability in us, and it is His hand that moves us.

Our praise should always be directed upward to God.

When we can surrender our hearts to God and be willing to die daily to self (as the Apostle Paul stated in I Corinthians 15:31 (KJV)), God can use us mightily. One of the quotes that God gave me early in my ministry was this: "If anything is going to happen through us, something must first happen to us." God desires to do great exploits through His children. However, we must present our bodies totally to Him. Romans 12:1 (NIV) says, "Therefore, I urge you, brothers, in view of God's mercy, to offer your bodies as living sacrifices, holy and pleasing to God—this is your spiritual act of worship." The word "offer" means to present for acceptance. We must yield our bodies to God in such a fashion that He is pleased with our offer. God never rejects a broken, contrite heart. Our hearts serve as an altar for our living sacrifice. The word "altar" denotes a place of slaughter. When we truly die to self, we have been slaughtered. The old self cannot be picked back up again. We have become a living sacrifice that is pleasing to God. We are holy because we are now set apart for God's use.

Romans 12:2 (NIV) says: "Do not conform any longer to the patterns of this world, but be transformed by the renewing of your mind." Our testimony is contradictory to God's nature when we conform to the patterns of this world. To conform means to adapt or blend in with the world. It means for us to compromise with the world's standards. We are in this world but not of it. We should not model ourselves after the patterns of this world. When we invite Jesus into our hearts, our minds are transformed and we are made new. This transformation is a complete metamorphosis. The old things have become new. As we renew our minds, we exchange them for the mind of Christ. What an exchange! Jesus comes inside and does a complete makeover. The change is recognizable by everyone.

Jesus tells us in His Word what we must do to be the

greatest in the Kingdom of God. We must *first* repent of our sin. The word "repent" means to turn from sin and turn to God—this is a 180 degree turn. When we repent of our sins, we are equipping our hearts for Kingdom living. The Kingdom of God is righteousness, peace, and joy in the Holy Spirit (Romans 14:17, KJV).

In the following passages, Jesus tells His disciples that they need to repent and become like little children. Jesus knew His disciples' hearts and He recognized that they needed to change. Matthew 18:1–3 (NIV) says: "At that time the disciples came to Jesus and asked, 'Who is the greatest in the Kingdom of Heaven?' He called a little child and had him stand among them. And He said: 'I tell you the truth, unless you change and become like little children, you will never enter the Kingdom of Heaven.'"

This change that Jesus is referring to is the complete metamorphosis that I mentioned previously; it is described in Romans 12:2. The disciples needed to change from a state of pride to a state of humility. When Jesus tells His disciples to change and become like little children, He is not indicating that they become childish but that they become childlike. To become childlike is to become Christlike. There are several innate characteristics of children that we need to exemplify if we are to become like little children. Children are trusting, dependent, carefree, and eager to please. God wants us to manifest these characteristics in our daily lives.

The *second* thing we need to do if we are going to be the greatest in the Kingdom of God is to respond in humility, like children. Matthew 18:4 (NIV) says: Therefore, whoever humbles himself like this child is the greatest in the Kingdom of Heaven. When we humble ourselves, we deny ourselves and we are of low rank and position. The condition of our hearts is totally yielded to Jesus.

The Bible says in I Peter 5:5b–6 (NIV): "All of you, clothe yourselves with humility toward one another, because 'God opposes the proud but gives grace to the humble.' Humble yourselves, therefore, under God's mighty hand, that He may lift you up in due time."

To clothe ourselves with humility means to be conscious of putting on lowliness, not exalting ourselves in pride. God fights against the proud—the boastful—but He gives grace, unmerited favor, to the humble. None of us wants God to fight against us; we all desire His grace.

When our hearts are humbled, we will want to serve others. Jesus says in Matthew 23:11–12 (KJV): "But he that is greatest among you shall be your servant. And whosoever shall exalt himself shall be abased; and he that shall humble himself shall be exalted." Jesus considers everyone who serves as the greatest in the Kingdom. A serving heart is indicative of a humble heart. The willingness to serve others means that we are eager to help meet the needs of others when it is in our power to help. It means making sacrifices regarding our own personal needs when necessary. We can be genuine servants only if we have a humble heart. Let's walk in humility. God will exalt us in due time.

The *third* thing we must do in order to be the greatest in the Kingdom of God is to receive little children like Jesus did. The word "receive" means to welcome with pleasure. We welcome little children because to be childlike is our new nature, and to be childlike is to be Christ-like. Jesus says in Matthew 18:5–6 (NIV): "And whoever welcomes a little child like this in My name welcomes Me. But if anyone causes one of these little ones who believe in Me to sin, it would be better for him to have a large millstone hung around his neck and to be drowned in the depths of the sea."

Jesus is serious about our treatment of little children. If we mistreat one of them and cause them to stumble, great punishment is imminent. There is no escaping the judgment of God if we mistreat little children or baby Christians by causing them to enter into sin. Our treatment of everyone is a matter of the condition of our hearts. We need to ask God to remove anything from our hearts that should not be present. As we clothe ourselves in humility like little children, we will have the correct mindset toward God's little ones—both children and those who are babes in the faith.

Consider this lesson in humility: I once read a story about Booker T. Washington, the famous black educator and the President of the Tuskegee Institute in Alabama. One day Mr. Washington was walking through an exclusive neighborhood that housed only white Americans. A white lady from the neighborhood approached him and asked him if he wanted to earn some extra money by chopping some wood for her and bringing it into the house. Mr. Washington agreed to chop the wood and do as the lady had suggested. When he brought the wood into the house, the lady's daughter recognized him as the profound educator at the Tuskegee Institute. After disclosing this information to her mother, the mother was totally embarrassed. She apologized over and over again to Mr. Washington for belittling him. He assured her that she had nothing to apologize for and that he had enjoyed chopping the wood. The lady reimbursed him for his labor as she had promised, and Mr. Washington departed. The lady was so impressed with his humility that she told all of her wealthy friends about him, and they donated thousands of dollars to the Tuskegee Institute. This story demonstrates the rewards of humility. When we humble ourselves before God, He will exalt us in due time.

As your own personal lesson in humility, perhaps you would like to invite Jesus into your heart to be your Lord and personal Savior. All you need to do is to pray the prayer below and contact a spiritual leader or clergy about being baptized; you need to become a part of a church and live a life for Jesus. The angels have a great celebration in heaven when you genuinely give your heart to Jesus. I invite you to do that by praying the prayer below, which is based upon Romans 10:9–10, and which will be repeated near the end of each chapter of this book:

THE SINNER'S PRAYER

Lord, Jesus, I am a sinner.

Please forgive me of all my sins and cleanse me from all unrighteousness.

I believe that You died for me on the cross and that You rose again.

Come now, Lord Jesus, and live Your life in me.

Fill me, Lord, with Your Holy Spirit.

Thank You, Lord, for saving me.

In Jesus' name I pray. Amen.

CHAPTER TWO

WINNING THROUGH CONFIDENCE

I can do all things through Christ who strengthens me.

PHILIPPIANS 4:13 (NKJV)

On a scale of one to ten, what is your confidence level? Do you believe the words that God says about you? We must grow in our confidence by believing what our Heavenly Father says about us. Growing in confidence is synonymous to growing in faith. According to the *New International Webster's Pocket Dictionary of the English Language,* the word "confidence" means to trust or to have faith in something or someone; it means to have self-assurance.

Here's my personal definition of "confidence":

- Seeing ourselves the way God sees us
- Believing in what God says about us
- Being sure of God's ability in us
- Having faith in God

My definition is predicated upon Psalm 139:14 (KJV), which says: "I will praise Thee; for I am fearfully and wonderfully made." Confidence involves believing what God says about us. We must believe that God has made us with honor and excellence. It is expedient to know that we are special in our Maker's eyes and that He has a plan and purpose for us to be successful in every area. God took the time to make us with great detail and design. We must now make the effort to honor His creation of us.

Before we can take strides to grow in our confidence, we must grasp a vision of what God wants us to achieve. Proverbs 29:18a (KJV) says: "Where there is no vision, the people perish." The word "vision" means divine revelation, or the act of seeing what is ahead. Our vision will enable us to do what God has called us to do, and it will enable us to stand firmly in our faith. If we don't have a vision of ourselves standing strongly, we will cast off restraint. We will not have a concrete picture of ourselves succeeding; thus, we will not have the confidence to move forward. In essence, we will see ourselves as being under our circumstances rather than above them. Having a vision means we will see ourselves as mighty and victorious in the Lord. God wants us walking above our circumstances and into the sphere that He has ordained for us to walk. In order to walk above our circumstances, we must have a vision. We must have the inner revelation from God that we can do all things through Christ, who gives us the strength (Philippians 4:13 NKJV).

Having a vision is paramount to developing confidence. Helen Keller was once asked, "What is worse than being born blind?" She replied, "Worse than being born blind is to have sight but no vision." Without vision, we cannot achieve the things that God has prepared for us. The greatest goal of Satan is to prevent our vision from becoming a reality. Vision involves dreaming and setting goals. Establishing goals is crucial in achieving God's vision for our lives. The word "goal," according to *Vine's Concise Dictionary of Bible Words,* comes from the Greek word, "skopeo," which means to look at something higher than yourself, or a mark on which to fix the eye. I heard someone say once that there is no sense in aiming for a target with no arrow in your bow. The arrow is our vision, which is cast higher than ourselves. The target is the goal that we reach. It is true that we never see the target a person aims at in life; we only see the target he hits. Our vision will not be visible to others until it is fulfilled; nevertheless, our success will be tangible, impacting when we launch our goals forward and when we actualize our dreams.

When I was a child, I dreamed of becoming a teacher. Even when family finances failed to align with my vision, my words remained positive. I continued to say, "I am going to be a teacher when I grow up." Coming from a family of fourteen children, money was definitely not in abundance; my mother, Mary Anna Ross, and my father, Thomas Bob Ross, persisted in assuring me that I would be a school teacher. Going to college was a goal that could be actualized only by a miracle. In actuality, that is what happened to me. Through prayer and hard work, I received a four-year academic scholarship to Lincoln University in Jefferson City, Missouri. After four years of college, I received my Bachelor of Science in Elementary Education, and began my first teaching job in St. Joseph, Missouri. Since that time, my dream of teaching has continued to blossom and unfold.

After teaching in the St. Joseph School District for fourteen years, God led me to a new assignment, with the same vision of teaching. On June 13, 1994, God called me to leave the classroom where I was teaching and enter into a bigger mission field of preaching and teaching His Word.

God does not always make His plans explicit to us. Nevertheless, I knew that He wanted me to leave the classroom and start an outreach ministry. He instructed me to do the things that He had already equipped me to do. Therefore, I started H.O.P.E. Outreach Ministries, Inc.—I began reading Bible storybooks to children at low-income apartment complexes. H.O.P.E. is an acronym for Helping Other People Excel. With the assistance of at least one hundred volunteers, we read to as many as 700 children each summer, and we witnessed many salvations and changed lives. In addition to the reading outreach, I taught Bible classes for women and men in these same housing complexes. I cannot even fathom the number of changed lives that have occurred as a result of this ministry. God's vision for us always involves building lives for the Kingdom of God.

I thank God for my husband, Charles, who was there by my side when I left the teaching profession and started the outreach ministry. He has been a constant supporter and encourager of my dreams and goals. Our sons—Charles, Jr., who was in tenth grade, and Andrew, who was in seventh grade—were very supportive. They asked no questions about why their mother was leaving the teaching profession and entering an uncertain, non-paying outreach ministry. They trusted God right along with my husband and me. God has done the miraculous because of our faith in Him.

In addition to the outreach ministry, I am now the Pastor and Founder of Hope Fellowship Church in St. Joseph, Missouri. I started this church—with the support and help of my husband, Charles—on June 4, 2009. All of my dreams and visions of becoming a teacher are enveloped in my role as a Pastor. God is doing great things in sending me people I can mold and develop spiritually for the Kingdom of God. My husband Charles, a former schoolteacher and coach, is right by my side, using his gifts and talents to fulfill God's purpose for his life. Our sons, Charles Jr. and Andrew—now adults—have always assisted me in the ministry. They live in other cities now, but they support me in every way possible. God has provided all that I need to accomplish His vision for my life. God's vision for us is made manifest as we serve Him faithfully. Colossians 3:23 (NKJV) says: "And whatever you do, do it heartily, as to the Lord and not to men." As we work faithfully for the Lord, He will disclose His plan for our lives. Knowing His plan enables us to serve with confidence.

Confidence and vision must co-exist. I remember when my confidence level rose one hundred percent. I was in the tenth grade at South Pemiscot High School, in Steele, Missouri. My English teacher had given us a writing assignment in which she indicated that she would select the best paper by a girl and the best paper by a boy. She would post them on a special bulletin board for everyone in the school to see. My confidence level rose because I knew that I had a passion for writing, and I knew that I had a great chance of my paper winning that contest. Therefore, I began to see myself as winning the contest.

When I went home from school that afternoon, I did my chores on the farm, and then I went straight to my room to work on my writing assignment. I remember staying up late into the evening working on that task. After several hours of grueling labor, the devil began to play tricks with my mind. I began to think thoughts of defeat, such as, "Do you think the teacher will choose your paper?" "You know that this is a predominately white school. Have the teachers at this school ever picked a black student's work to acknowledge their success?" "Why do you think she will pick your paper? You are poor and black." In my mind, I agreed with everything the devil was saying. So why was I working so hard? Right at the moment of my deepest low, God spoke to me. He said, "I did not create you as an inferior; you can do that work. So do it!"

I literally heard my Heavenly Father's voice speak these words to me; the moment was so profound that it changed my life. There was no mistake about it. God had given me confidence, and I have never been the same since that night. With those divine words, I grabbed a new sheet of paper, and I wrote that composition with all of my ability. I now had a renewed confidence, and a vision of winning the contest.

The next day I submitted my paper to the teacher. I was very nervous, yet confident that my paper would be chosen as the best paper by a girl. It took the teacher about three days to grade the papers and return them to the students, posting the best ones. When I entered the classroom on that third day, I saw the special bulletin board with two papers posted. "Could one of those papers be mine?" I asked myself.

As I drew closer, I saw my paper was one of the two chosen. How excited I was! The boy whose paper was chosen was the richest boy in the school, and here I was, probably the poorest girl in the school. God is good! On this particular day, I saw myself in a whole new light. I saw myself as a person of great potential. I now had the confidence to make plans for college and to set my heart on anything that God had for me to accomplish. My low self-esteem had become God-esteem. I am valuable because of God's ability in me.

A crucial point to remember is that Satan is a liar. He will make us feel contrary to what God's Word says about us. Remember to stand your ground and speak God's Word with confidence. We must not allow fear to reside in us or inhibit our success. We must remember that God has not given us a spirit of fear. He has given us power, love, and a sound mind (II Timothy 1:7 KJV).

Many times our dreams are dashed because of fear. Whenever we are afraid, we need to remember that God did not give us that spirit. It is from the enemy. So let's rebuke the fear in the name of Jesus. We must see ourselves as mighty in the Lord. I have heard it said that the acronym for fear is:

False
Evidence
Appearing
Real

Isn't this acronym true? Fear is false evidence appearing real. Since Satan is a liar and a deceiver, he will camouflage false information to make it appear real. For this reason, it is imperative to stand firm in the truth of God's word. We must hold on to our confidence and remain constant in our vision.

Since confidence is necessary in the temporal world, it is overwhelmingly significant in the heavenly realm. When we consider our spiritual lives, our confidence will provide three things: heavenly reward, heavenly readiness, and heavenly reassurance.

HEAVENLY REWARD

In the spiritual realm, one of the things that our confidence provides is our heavenly reward. Hebrew 10:35–36 (KJV) says: "Cast not away therefore your confidence, which hath great recompense of reward. For ye have need of patience, that, after ye have done the will of God, ye might receive the promise."

The confidence that I learned in the tenth grade when my paper was selected as the best paper by a girl has taught me a great deal about perseverance. I could have given up that night, when the enemy was doing battle in my mind, trying to make me feel inferior. Instead, I choose to believe what God says about me. God did not create me as an inferior being; He created me as a capable, valiant warrior for Him. I am fearfully and wonderfully made.

I now have the confidence to persevere in order to receive the heavenly reward that God has promised. Perseverance is the ability to continue in the midst of difficult trials. We must be steadfast and immovable, even when powerful punches are coming our way. The blows of the enemy should not deter us from pressing on toward our heavenly reward. The Bible says in II Timothy 4:18 (KJV) that the Lord will rescue us from every evil attack and He will bring us safely to His Heavenly Kingdom. The word "rescue" means to save or to deliver. God is our deliverer and our salvation.

Knowing that God will rescue us, it is imperative to keep our focus on Him. Hebrews 12:2a (NIV) says: "Let us fix our eyes on Jesus, the author and perfecter of our faith." Our faith begins and ends with Jesus; therefore, we must let Him fight our battles. It might appear convenient sometimes to take matters into our own hands. Perhaps this tendency causes us to lash out at other people or say hurtful things. God has mapped out a path for us. As we fix our eyes on Jesus, we become committed to His plan. With our eyes fixed on Jesus, we won't take another route in fighting our battles. Jesus is our mighty warrior. He fights our battles for us and through us.

In receiving our heavenly reward, we must learn to press on to achieve our goal. Philippians 3:12–13 (NIV) says, "Not that I have already obtained all this or have already been made perfect, but I press on to take hold of that for which Christ Jesus took hold of me. Brothers, I do not consider myself yet to have taken hold of it. But one thing I do: Forgetting what is behind and straining toward what is ahead." Holding on to the past can deter us from achieving our heavenly reward. The baggage of past hurts or painful relationships can weigh us down, swaying us off course. The effect can be gradual, but soon enough we find ourselves off the path that God has charted for us.

Just like the Apostle Paul had to press on, it is necessary for us to press on toward the mark of our high calling of heaven. The Bible says in Philippians 3:14 (NLT): "I press on to reach the end of the race and receive the heavenly prize for which God, through Christ Jesus, is calling us." God is summoning or inviting us to heaven because it is His ultimate plan for our lives.

HEAVENLY READINESS

Another thing that our spiritual confidence provides is heavenly readiness. Since I am certain that heaven is my destination, I walk in readiness every day. I dress accordingly in my expectation of seeing Jesus face to face. My readiness is based upon the confidence that I am born again. My salvation prepares me for the trip. I can recall when my husband, Charles, and I were dating. I would dress in accordance to where he was taking me on our date. If we were going to a football game, I would dress in jeans, a t-shirt or sweatshirt, and tennis shoes. If we were going to church, I would wear a dress and slightly high heels. The point is that before Charles ever arrived, I prepared myself for our excursion.

Heavenly readiness is similar. We know that Jesus is returning soon. Are we dressed for the trip? Our attire is our garment of salvation. Since we are saved, we know that we are going to heaven with Jesus when He returns. This hope keeps us waiting and watching in confidence. Hebrew 10:37 (NIV) says: "For in just a very little while, 'He who is coming will come and will not delay.'"

I mentioned earlier that I am from a family of fourteen children, and I am next to the oldest in birth order. At a certain point, there were nine of us getting on the school bus at the same time. With such a large number of children catching the bus, all of us had to be certain that clothes were laid out the night before in order to expedite getting dressed the next morning. One of my responsibilities was to supervise this preparation. I don't recall any of us ever missing the bus. Preparation was the key. We knew that the bus was coming at a certain time, and we took necessary strides to be ready.

We must do the same thing in our spiritual readiness for the return of Jesus Christ. Since we don't know the time or date that our Lord will return, we must be ready at all times. The Bible says in I John 2:28 (NIV): "And now, dear children, continue in Him, so that when He appears we may be confident and unashamed before Him at His coming." Our confidence rests in the fact that we are steadfast in our walk with the Lord. As we walk with Jesus, He walks with us. When He returns, we will be confident and unashamed at His coming for us.

Heavenly readiness is sustained by our knowing that God has a calling and purpose for our lives. According to *Vine's Concise Dictionary of Bible Words,* the word "calling," which comes from the Hebrew word *qara* and the Greek word *kaleo,* means:

- The act of specifying a name
- The act of specifying a primary characteristic; such as that the name "Jacob" means "deceiver" (Genesis 27:36)

- The act of summoning or inviting to a vocation or destination
- God's plan or purpose for us

God says in Jeremiah 29:11 (NLT), "For I know the plans I have for you," says the Lord. "They are plans for good and not for disaster, to give you a future and a hope." Those words are consoling. God wants the best for us. Our calling will ensure that God's best will materialize in our lives. As we fulfill God's plan for us, our obedience will maintain our heavenly readiness. Jesus says in Luke 19:13b (KJV): "Occupy till I come."

Jesus wants us to occupy until He comes. He wants us to be occupied with using the gifts and abilities that He has entrusted us with until He returns again. This instruction means that Jesus wants us to do the things that He has called us to do without getting side-tracked. We must stay focused.

The Bible says in Ephesians 2:10 (NIV), "For we are God's workmanship, created in Christ Jesus to do good works, which God prepared in advance for us to do." There are no surprises with God. He prepared before the foundation of world what we are called to do. God knew in advance what we would be doing this very day. It is up to us to make the next move. God has given us a free will. Our assignment is not forced. We fulfill our calling out of love for our Lord.

HEAVENLY REASSURANCE

The third thing that confidence provides is heavenly reassurance. We can be sure that we are going to heaven. When I was in college, I thought that I was sure that I was going to heaven until I was approached by a radical believer in Jesus.

This young man was so bold and fearless that he would unashamedly approach an entire line of hungry college students. He would look them in the eyes as they waited to be served in the cafeteria and ask, "Are you saved?" Everybody else laughed and devalued his question, thinking he was somewhat insane. But I took it seriously. I knew that I loved Jesus. I was baptized at the age of eleven, and I attended church every Sunday. But was I going to heaven? Somehow the way this guy asked this question caused me to examine myself with renewed conviction.

Since I was under a new quest to be certain of my salvation, I began to fast and pray—imploring God to reveal truth to me. I wanted to be sure that I was saved and that I was going to heaven. Almost in a state of panic, I began to read the New Testament Scriptures, seeking God for answers. At the conclusion of reading the four Gospels, I went on a three-day fast; I was sincerely seeking God for an answer. On the evening of day three of my fast, God revealed Himself to me. As I was sleeping in the top bunk of my bed in an apartment that I was renting in Jefferson City, Missouri, God revealed Himself to me in the form of light. Light filled the top bunk of my room. My roommate was sleeping below and she was totally unaware of what was happening. God's Shekinah glory—the visible manifestation of His presence—filled the room, and I knew that God Himself was there with me. I lay there motionless and in awe of God's presence. I could only say, repeatedly, "God, you are real. You are here with me. You are so real!"

God did not speak audibly to me that evening, but His presence gave me the assurance that I was going to heaven. I was confident that I was His child. God's presence revealed to me that I was saved and that I was heaven bound. Since that time as a twenty-year-old college student, I have never questioned my salvation nor have I thought twice about whether or not I am going to heaven. My confidence that I am a Christian reassures me of being with God forever in heaven. Being certain that heaven is my eternal address is due to my faith in Jesus Christ. The same is true for any believer. Jesus told Nicodemus that he must be born again. In John 3:3 (NIV) Jesus says, "I tell you the truth, no one can see the Kingdom of God unless he is born again." To be born again means that we invite Jesus into our hearts and He comes to live on the inside of us. He gives us a spiritual rebirth with God-given DNA. We become God's children and He is our heavenly Father. As born-again Christians, our character must mirror that of our Heavenly Father. We must act like Him since He is our Father. When we invite Jesus into our heart to be our Lord and Savior, we are born again and we are going to heaven. That is our heavenly reassurance.

Heavenly reassurance means that we walk in faith, believing that heaven is our home and that we must not depart from our belief. Despite the distractions, we must stay focused and keep the faith. In Hebrews 10:38 (NIV), God says: "But my righteous one will live by faith. And if he shrinks back, I will not be pleased with him." God does not want us to pull back from our faith because we please Him by our faith. It is natural to want to please those we love. If we truly love God, we will want to please Him with our faith. Hebrews 10:39 (NIV) says: "But we are not of those who shrink back and are destroyed, but of those who believe and are saved."

We are assured of heaven if we believe and are saved. Salvation assures us that heaven will be our home. Therefore, we can wait for our blessed hope, Jesus Christ, to return. At the conclusion of our lives, we can say as the Apostle Paul said in II Timothy 4:7–8 (NIV): "I have fought the good fight, I have finished the race, I have kept the faith. Now there is in store for me the crown of righteousness, which the Lord, the righteous Judge, will award to me on that day—and not only to me, but also to all who have longed for His appearing."

Living the Christian life means fighting the good fight. Every fight might not appear to be good, but the outcome is good; we are victorious because our aim is heavenward and our confidence is secure. We have a reward in store. Do you long for the appearing of Jesus Christ? Do you find yourself getting restless in anticipation for His return? The time will come when Jesus will come back. Those of us who have invited Him into our hearts will receive a crown of righteousness to wear in heaven. We will receive our glorified bodies that will never get sick again or have any pain. Everything will be made new. If you want to have the confidence of making heaven your home, you must have Jesus in your heart. Just pray The Sinner's Prayer below and invite Jesus into your heart. Praying this prayer will ensure you that heaven will be your reward. Please follow up by contacting a Pastor for water baptism and membership.

THE SINNER'S PRAYER

Lord, Jesus, I am a sinner.

Please forgive me of all my sins and cleanse me from all unrighteousness.

I believe that You died for me on the cross and that You rose again.

Come now, Lord Jesus, and live Your life in me.

Fill me, Lord, with Your Holy Spirit.

Thank You, Lord, for saving me.

In Jesus' name I pray. Amen.

CHAPTER THREE

WINNING THROUGH MATTERS OF THE HEART

Create in me a clean heart, O God, and renew a steadfast spirit within me.

PSALM 51:10 (NKJV)

Remember, we are in this race to win it. We cannot be victorious if our heart is impure before God. Man looks at the outward appearance, but God looks at the heart. Our hearts are our innermost selves. When we ask God to create clean hearts in us, we are asking Him to "un-sin" us. We are asking God to take all of the sin out of our hearts so that we can stand before Him entirely pure. After David committed adultery with Bathsheba, Uriah the Hittite's wife, he realized his sin before God (I Kings 15:5). Up to this point, David had pleased the Lord in his walk before Him. After Nathan the prophet confronted David regarding his sin, he prayed the following prayer of confession: "Create in me a clean heart, O God, and renew a steadfast spirit within me" (Psalm 51:10 NKJV).

David desired to be right in the sight of God. He knew that he was unable to fix his heart and thus, turned to God to do this miraculous task. We are like David. When we sin, we are incapable of "un-sinning" ourselves. God is the only one who can help us. Although David's sin extended to Bathsheba and Uriah, his greatest responsibility was to God. He wanted to make things right. He wanted to be reconciled in his relationship with God. In Psalm 51:4 (NLT), David prayed: "Against you, and you alone, have I sinned; I have done what is evil in your sight. You will be proved right in what you say, and your judgment against me is just."

Can you sense David's heart of repentance? Maybe this situation reminds you of a great sin you have committed. You can be forgiven by God. Any of us can be cleansed by the blood of Jesus. All we have to do is confess our sins before God and He will forgive us. The Bible says in I John 1:9 (NIV): "If we confess our sins, He is faithful and just and will forgive us our sins and purify us from all unrighteousness."

None of us are out of the scope of God's forgiveness, and neither was David. He prayed in Psalm 51:7–8 (NLT): "Purify me from my sins, and I will be clean; wash me, and I will be whiter than snow. Oh, give me back my joy again; you have broken me—now let me rejoice."

When we have sinned against God, others and ourselves, we lose our joy. Our heart becomes discombobulated; we are torn asunder. The only solution is confession and repentance. Confession means that we admit our wrong and maintain a Godly sorrow; repentance means that we turn totally from our sin and go in the direction of God's righteousness.

A HEART OF FORGIVENESS

If we are in this race to win it, we must get rid of all unforgiveness that plagues our heart. I heard someone say once, "When a friend makes a mistake, don't rub it in. Rub it out." This adage sums up the meaning of forgiveness. The term, which comes from the Hebrew word *calach* and the Greek word *aphiemi*, is defined below from *Vine's Concise Dictionary of Bible Words*:

- The act of pardoning
- The act of releasing
- The act of sending away
- The act of cancelling a debt
- The act of giving up all claims for resentment and revenge

Hebrew 9:22b (English Standard Version) says: "Without the shedding of blood, there is no forgiveness of sins." Jesus died once and for all so that our sins could be forgiven. His blood paid the price for all of our wrongdoings. Since Jesus has forgiven us, we must forgive others. Jesus tells us in the Lord's Prayer, found in Matthew 6:12 (NKJV): "And forgive us our debts, as we forgive our debtors." This verse is asking God to forgive us of our sins as we forgive those who have sinned against us. A debt is something owed. Forgiveness is synonymous to the cancelling of a debt.

There is an Old Testament account of some of David's children entering into unforgiveness. David's oldest son, Amnon, who is the half-brother of David's daughter Tamar, enters into bitter conflict. Amnon begins to lust after Tamar and determines in his heart to have sex with her. He pretends to be ill and requests to have Tamar come and serve food to him. When she arrives, he asks her to feed him the food that she has prepared. The story unfolds in II

Samuel 13:11–12, 14 (NIV) as follows: "But when she took it to him to eat, he grabbed her and said, 'Come to bed with me, my sister.' 'Don't, my brother!' she said to him. 'Don't force me. Such a thing should not be done in Israel! Don't do this wicked thing.' But he refused to listen to her, and since he was stronger than she, he raped her."

What a great offense against Tamar, the half-sister of Amnon. Such wickedness was a disgrace to Israel and the house of David. Amnon deceived Tamar, overpowered her by raping her, and took her virginity. After he had violated her, he hated her and himself. The Bible says in II Samuel 13:15–16 (NIV): "Then Amnon hated her with intense hatred. In fact, he hated her more than he had loved her. Amnon said to her, 'Get up and get out!' 'No!' she said to him. 'Sending me away would be a greater wrong than what you have already done to me.' But he refused to listen to her."

Since Tamar was no longer a virgin, she could not be offered by her father to a potential husband. Her life was over. This humongous sin against Tamar caused her full brother, Absalom, who was David's son, to intervene. II Samuel 13:20 (NIV) says: "Her brother Absalom said to her, 'Has that Amnon, your brother, been with you? Be quiet now, my sister; he is your brother. Don't take this thing to heart.' And Tamar lived in her brother Absalom's house a desolate woman."

We can probably understand Absalom's stance in protecting his sister, Tamar. However, the bitterness and hatred that followed led to a disastrous outcome. Not only was Absalom angered over this great sin, but Tamar's father, King David, was equally outraged. II Samuel 13:21–22 (NIV) says: "When King David heard all this, he was furious. Absalom never said a word to Amnon, either good or bad; he hated Amnon because he had disgraced his sister Tamar."

The Bible tells us to get rid of bitterness because it can develop a root that runs deep into our heart. Ephesians 4:31 (KJV) says: "Let all bitterness, and wrath, and anger, and clamor, and evil speaking, be put away from you, with all malice." The word "malice" means to have ill will against another and to desire to inflict harm. Although Absalom never said a word to Amnon for about two years, he harbored much bitterness and hatred in his heart. The anger and bitterness that Absalom stored in his heart transpired into murder. Absalom, Tamar's brother, executed a plot to have Amnon murdered.

The Bible says in II Samuel 13:28–29 (NIV), "Absalom ordered his men, 'Listen! When Amnon is in high spirits from drinking wine and I say to you, "Strike Amnon down," then kill him. Don't be afraid. Have not I given you this order? Be strong and brave. So Absalom's men did to Amnon what Absalom had ordered. Then all the king's sons got up, mounted their mules and fled."

Absalom took matters into his own hands rather than giving them to God. He had his brother, Amnon, murdered. David, Absalom's father, was heartbroken over the dysfunctional behavior in his family. But more heartbreak followed in other instances.

Perhaps someone has wronged you and you have justifiable cause to seek revenge. God admonishes us to leave revenge to Him. He says in Romans 12:19 (KJV), "Dearly beloved, avenge not yourselves, but rather give place unto wrath: for it is written, Vengeance is mine; I will repay, saith the Lord."

No matter how carefully orchestrated a human plot to get revenge might be, God does the best job of issuing payback. Remember, everyone reaps what he or she sows. Therefore, let God perform the dispersing of payment for wrongs done against you.

FORGIVE YOUR NEIGHBOR

To forgive others is a discipline that our Lord wants us to exercise. When we don't forgive others, that person is holding us hostage. God wants us to forgive our neighbor. Who is our neighbor? Our neighbor is anyone in our sphere of influence that we can help. Since our neighbor is in close proximity to us, that person has the likelihood of irritating us or rubbing us the wrong way. A teenage girl in our Vacation Bible School class became annoyed because her fellow classmate, who was a teenage boy, kept pestering her. He kept teasing her and talking non-stop. So she reached over and slapped him on the side of his face. When asked by the teacher why she had struck her fellow classmate, she replied, "He pushed the wrong button and I couldn't take it anymore."

Yes, there are times when people push us beyond limit, and internally we feel like taking actions that make us feel good for the moment. Nevertheless, there are always consequences for our actions. Through prayer and guidance from the Holy Spirit, we can train ourselves to be more patient with others and find ways to ignore offensive behavior no matter how petty or serious it might appear to be. The Bible says in Colossians 3:13 (KJV), "Forbearing one another, and forgiving one another, if any man have a quarrel against any: even as Christ forgave you, so also do ye."

Just think of how annoying we might appear before God each day. He forgives us for our childish ways, and He continues to shower us with His blessings. Sometimes I find myself getting impatient with immature adults. God has taught me that not everyone is at the same level of spiritual growth. Regardless of the fact that a person may have been a Christian for many years, that person may have had a great deal of barriers or baggage to work through. Who are we to judge? Our job is to love them and not judge them. We must ask God to help us overcome our judgmental attitude toward those who might be on a different maturity level. We never know what obstacles might have contributed to that person's stunted spiritual maturity. Perhaps we can ask God to use us to help escalate our neighbor's growth and spiritual development.

The Bible says in Ephesians 4:2 (KJV) that we should be completely humble and gentle and patient, bearing with one another in love. I was convicted by the Holy Spirit several months ago in dealing with a person who was very immature but possessed an outward display of authority. In observing her, one would think that she was quite experienced and mature in the Lord. This particular person was about fifty years old, and she had all the spiritual language. Nevertheless, I noticed that she was always making poor choices, and she never could manage to maintain relationships, male or female. Outwardly, this individual appeared to be mature, but socially, spiritually, and intellectually she lacked the rationale for making common sense decisions.

I approached her one day because of some problems that had surfaced due to her poor decision-making abilities. I was under the assumption that she should have known better for making the choices that she made because they affected others around her. From that conversation, I learned a great deal about this lady. She had practically raised herself from childhood. Her outward performance was for survival. This pretense was how she had managed to survive all of these years. She possessed minimal skills for relationship-building because she had no role models in her life. Many people alienated themselves from her because she had a tendency to push them away.

God disclosed so much to me about this dear lady, who was craving love and understanding. I was not aware of this earlier because I was judging her on her outward pretense of maturity and authority. In my meeting with her, I learned that she could not perform any higher than her experiences, background, and mental capacity would allow. God taught me a lesson in love. I learned to be patient with her and not expect more than she could yield. A key point to remember is that we must get to know the people that we call our neighbors. Things are not always the way they appear. Love will propel us to investigate the situation at hand and understand motives; love will motivate us to be willing to forgive with a sincere heart.

In forgiving our neighbor, our neighbor could be a family member because that person is in our sphere of influence. Anyone in our sphere of influence will have the potential to offend us in one way or another. For this reason, our hearts must be poised to forgive. I am reminded of a story I heard about a father and son who had a bitter dispute. Hurtful words were exchanged—some of which seemed too painful to be forgiven. The father thought about the harsh argument and sought ways to reconcile with his son. But he didn't know where he was or how to reach him. Suddenly, the Holy Spirit impressed upon his heart to put an article in the local newspaper. He obeyed. Here is what the article said, "Dear Paco, please meet me in front of the newspaper office downtown at noon on Saturday. I am sorry for everything that I said. All is forgiven; I love you. Sincerely, your father."

The newspaper reported that on that Saturday at noon, 800 young men by the name of Paco showed up seeking forgiveness from their fathers. Only one father had the courage to write this article and his son did appear in front of the newspaper office. The Bible tells us in Ephesians 4:3 that we should make every effort to keep the unity of the Spirit through the bond of peace. This father took the steps to promote peace as he sought reconciliation through the medium of the local newspaper.

Another neighbor that we might be reluctant to mention is our enemy. Yes, we all have enemies at one time or another. How do we handle our enemies? Jesus said the following in Matthew 5:44 (NIV), "But I tell you: Love your enemies and pray for those who persecute you." This is a tall order to fill. The only way this can be accomplished is by drawing from the well of the Holy Spirit that is in our heart. One of the fruit of the Spirit is love. Love is the primary attribute of our Heavenly Father. As God's children, we have the seed of love inside us. The only possible way to love our enemy is by the power of God's love operating within us.

Jesus is the perfect example of how we should love our enemies. He was persecuted, beaten, and nailed to a cross. Ultimately, He died for our sins. Not once in the entire ordeal did He curse His enemies or neglect His mission. He could have abandoned the cross without paying the penalty for our sins. However, He chose to remain silent for us and demonstrated the greatest act of being a true neighbor—He died for His friends. John 15:13 (New Living Translation) says, "There is no greater love than to lay down one's life for one's friends."

A HEART OF LOVE

A heart of love is one that loves at all times. I am reminded of my love for my husband, Charles, and our two sons, Charlie Jr. and Andrew. There is nothing that they could do to change my love for them. My love is unconditional. Love is a fact, not a fable. The Bible says in I John 4:16b (NIV), "God is love. Whoever lives in love lives in God, and God in him."

In order for us to love, God must be our dwelling place, and we must be His. The act is reciprocal. God is in us and we are in Him. Believe me, it takes that kind of relationship in order for real love to exist. In today's world there is so much counterfeit love—love that is based on conditions. Real love has no conditions. Real love is known only by the actions it prompts. We can give without loving, but we can't love without giving. The kind of love that defines God is "agape love," which is defined below from *Vine's Concise Dictionary of Bible Words*:

- Comes from the Greek word "agape"; expresses the nature of God
- Divine love that shows God's love for man; man's love for God; and man's love for man
- Voluntarily enslaving oneself to God

Jesus defines agape love in Matthew 22:37–38 (NIV) when He says, "Love the Lord your God with all your heart and with all your soul and with all your mind. This is the first and greatest commandment."

When we manifest the kind of love that Jesus is talking about in these verses, we will treat everyone with a loving attitude; we will not bring harm to our friends, family, or ourselves. No one will have to remind us about the proper way to behave, because God's love is on the inside of us and we are on the inside of God.

Jesus continues to say in Matthew 22:39–40 (NIV), "And the second is like it: 'Love your neighbor as yourself.' All the Law and the Prophets hang on these two commandments." All of the Ten Commandments rest on these two commandments of love. When love is innate, we don't have to be reminded about how to treat someone, because love will navigate us. When real love resonates in our hearts, we won't steal from our neighbor or take his wife. We will want to please God in all that we do; we will read our Bible and spend time with God in a desperate fashion. A spiritual hunger will remain in our souls. We will likewise have the motivation to love ourselves.

I have not always loved myself. Poor self-esteem is something with which I can identify. God has delivered me from thinking that I am inferior or from thinking that I am incapable of doing what He has called me to do. On a daily basis, I have to remind myself that God did not create me as an inferior, and that I am fearfully and wonderfully made. There are certain things that we must know for sure if we are going to be successful in life. One of those things is that God is a God of love, and He loves us so much that He would not create us to be a failure. Failure might occur in our lives, but we are not failures. Every one of us was created to succeed and God is no respecter of persons—meaning God has no favorites.

Something else we must consider in loving ourselves is that before the foundation of the world, God had a plan for us. He created us for a purpose in the entire scheme of the world. As an analogy, consider a jigsaw puzzle. The puzzle is made by cutting a picture into pieces of uneven shapes; these shapes must be put together to form the picture in its entirety. God saw the whole picture before the world was formed. We are just one piece of the puzzle that will make this world a better place. My role as Pastor and teacher might not be as big as someone else's role, but it is just as important. No one can complete my piece of the puzzle but me. If I don't do my part, it will not be accomplished. I like the statement that says, "When God created me, He threw away the mold." For this illustration, that statement is true. There is no one else in the entire world like you and me. Each one of us is an individual with unique gifts and abilities. Therefore, let's love ourselves with the love of Jesus Christ.

Real love is always sincere, whether we are loving our neighbor or loving ourselves. The word "sincere" comes from the old English word meaning "without wax." In ancient times, it was customary for many merchants to make pottery. Over time the pottery would develop cracks. Dishonest merchants would put wax over the cracks to conceal the imperfection. Honest merchants whose pottery did not have cracks would put a sign on their pottery that said "without wax," which meant that no cracks were in their product. In order to test the pottery, one could hold it up to the light, which would reveal the cracks.

The same principle can be applied to test genuine love. Pretentious love will be revealed by the cracks of worldliness and carnality. The Fruit of the Spirit will not be evident in that person's life. If a person says that they love you with all of their heart, hold them up to the light of Jesus Christ. If that person has the qualities of Jesus, then you can be confident of their love for you. Jesus is always the measuring rod for true love. Jesus says in John 13:34–35 (NKJV), "A new commandment I give to you. That you love one another; as I have loved you, that you also love one another. By this, all will know that you are My disciples, if you have love for one another." We don't have to go around wearing a badge that says we are disciples; it will be known by the love we have for one another.

REMOVE THE CLUTTER

In our homes we do spring cleaning. Why not do some spring cleaning in our hearts and remove some of the clutter that can accumulate? David prays a prayer for God to examine his heart and remove the clutter. David was truly devoted to God and he wanted to walk in a pure manner. He prayed in Psalm 139:23–24 (NIV), "Search me, O God, and know my heart; test me and know my anxious thoughts. See if there is any offensive way in me, and lead me in the way everlasting." When God does a search, He is thorough in His findings. He is fair and honest; He will reveal those things that can only be removed by genuine repentance. We must have a sorrowful heart and sincerely want the sin to be removed; sin must be repulsive to us. Our desire must be for God to lead us down a pure and holy path that is pleasing to Him. Jesus shed His blood on Calvary for us so that all we have to do is ask forgiveness for our sins. I John 1:9 (NIV) says, "If we confess our sins, He is faithful and just and will forgive us our sins and purify us from all unrighteousness." God has promised in His Word that He will forgive us of our sins when we confess them before Him.

There was a person who was praying for God to remove sin and undesirable traits from his heart. So he prayed the following prayer: "Lord, take the cobwebs out of my life." Shortly after he prayed that prayer, he heard God say to him, "Get rid of the spider." The spider of course is the source of the cobwebs. What is the source of your sin? Is it lust? Or is it greed? God wants us to flee sin and flee the source of that sin, which originates in the heart. When we hide God's word in our heart, we will not sin against God (Psalm 119:11 KJV).

David prayed another prayer for spiritual renewal. It is found in Psalm 51:10 (NKJV) that says, "Create in me a clean heart, O God, and renew a steadfast spirit within me." The incident that precipitated this prayer was when the prophet Nathan came to David after he had committed adultery with Bathsheba. David recognized his sin and desired a new heart and a new spirit from God. He wanted the old nature of sin to be totally eradicated. Only God can create something new from something old. He wanted God to un-sin him. The word "renew" means to exchange. David wanted to exchange his old heart of sin for a new heart of righteousness that was pleasing to God. Only God could fashion a clean heart and a new spirit in David. He wanted his inner man to be steadfast and immovable. The power of the Holy Spirit is crucial in keeping us on the right path. David desired that the Holy Spirit would not be taken away from him. The Holy Spirit is our enabling agent who keeps us walking in holiness.

In the Old Testament, the Holy Spirit did not dwell with everyone. He only abided with prophets, priests, and kings. David was anointed by God to be king; therefore, the Holy Spirit dwelt with him and upon him. David treasured the working of the Holy Spirit in his life, and he recognized the importance of the power of the Holy Spirit in fulfilling God's plans for him.

Today, the Holy Spirit dwells with every believer who is born again. "Born again" means that we have invited Jesus into our hearts, asking Him to be our Lord and personal Savior. At that moment, the Holy Spirit comes inside of us and will be with us forever. The Holy Spirit is our "paraclete," which means that He comes alongside of us to be our helper. We truly cannot make it without the Holy Spirit. The Holy Spirit helps us to guard our hearts from sin. Proverbs 4:23 (KJV) says, "Keep thy heart with all diligence; for out of it are the issues of life." Just think how important our hearts are. Our hearts are central to our emotions and innermost thoughts. God looks at the heart, whereas man looks at the outward appearance. Since our hearts are so important, God wants us to guard what goes inside.

The word "guard" is a military term. We must stand at attention and let nothing distract us. Let's swat away anything that is contrary to the nature and will of God. Our heart is the wellspring of life, meaning that it is the source of life. Matthew 12:34-35 (NIV) says, "Out of the overflow of the heart the mouth speaks. The good man brings good things out of the good stored up in him, and the evil man brings evil things out of the evil stored up in him." If you really want to know what is in a person's heart, just listen to their words. We can be squeezed like toothpaste. What comes out of our mouths when we are squeezed? Do kind words come forth? Or do evil and profane words come forth? Whatever is stored up will come forth.

In removing the clutter, we must remember—just as David recognized—that we must take off the old nature. Colossians 3:5 (NIV) says, "Put to death, therefore, whatever belongs to your earthly nature: sexual immorality, impurity, lust, evil desires, and greed, which is idolatry." We put our old nature to death by failing to feed the flesh. By the power of the Holy Spirit, we crucify the flesh, which means we put it to death. When we are truly walking in the Spirit, we won't have the same sinful desires. If desires from the old nature attempt to surface, resist them in the name of Jesus. The Apostle Paul said in I Corinthians 15:31 (KJV), "I die daily."

If we are Christians, we have already crucified the sinful nature. Galatians 5:24–25 (KJV) says, "And they that are Christ's have crucified the flesh with the affections and lusts. If we live in the spirit, let us also walk in the Spirit." In other words, let's not get ahead of the Spirit or walk out of step with the Spirit. We must match our steps with the steps of the Spirit. It is paramount to remember that we have two natures: the Spirit nature and the fleshly or sinful nature. The two natures are at constant war with each other. The nature that will win is the one we feed the most. If we feed or nurture the Spirit, then the Spirit will win. However, if we feed the flesh or sinful nature, the sinful nature will win. Therefore, let's feed the Holy Spirit by staying in the word of God and by living the life that God has ordained for us.

Getting rid of the old nature involves getting rid of childishness. The Apostle Paul says in I Corinthians 13:11 (NKJV), "When I was a child, I spoke as a child, I understood as a child, I thought as a child; but when I became a man, I put away childish things." The characteristics of a child include that it whines a great deal, throws fits of anger, and is self-centered. I pray that these qualities do not epitomize your Christian behavior. If so, please put them away. That is what God's word says. I have known childish Christians who have a critical spirit. They criticize everything and everyone. Whenever I see that behavior in a Christian, I know that immaturity resides in the heart of that individual. It is time to put that behavior aside and grow into Christian maturity.

As we take off the old nature, we must put on new clothing. Colossians 3:10 and 12 (NIV) says, "Put on the new self, which is being renewed in knowledge in the image of its Creator. Therefore, as God's chosen people, holy and dearly loved, clothe yourselves with compassion, kindness, humility, gentleness, and patience." When we put on our clothing on a daily basis, it is deliberate. We might even lay out our garments ahead of time in order to be prepared. Whatever the case, we put on our clothing in a systematic and orchestrated manner. The same must be true with spiritual clothing as we determine in our hearts that we will walk in love and compassion, demonstrating the very nature of God. As we walk in our spiritual clothing, we are conformed to the image of Jesus. When people see us, we look like Jesus. Then we are really dressed to kill! We kill the old nature.

When we are in Christ, we are a new creation; the old has

gone, and the new has come (II Corinthians 5:17 KJV). The key is to be *in* Christ. The preposition "in" means that we are contained by, surrounded by, or covered by something or someone. Does Jesus totally engulf us? When we are totally surrounded by Jesus, we are a new creation. The old nature has gone and the new nature has come. Praise God!

To give an illustration, there was a soap manufacturer and a Pastor walking down the street together. As they walked in a poor part of the neighborhood, the soap manufacturer remarked, "The Gospel you preach must not do much good. I look around and see all of this sin in this neighborhood. There is a lot of wickedness in the world."

The Pastor did not respond immediately but continued to walk and talk with the soap manufacturer. After a while the two men came upon some dirty children playing outside in front of their apartment building. The Pastor then remarked, "I see that soap hasn't done much good in this neighborhood. Look at those dirty children and all of the dirty people. As a matter of fact, there are so many dirty people in the whole world."

The soap manufacturer became outraged and shouted, "Well, soap is only useful when applied. It's available; they just have to apply it."

The Pastor cheerfully replied, "That is exactly the point of the Gospel message. The Gospel is available, but it must be applied!"

If you do not know the Lord Jesus as your Lord and personal Savior and you want to apply the Gospel by inviting Jesus into your heart, just pray The Sinner's Prayer below and contact a church for baptism and follow-up.

THE SINNER'S PRAYER

Lord, Jesus, I am a sinner.

Please forgive me of all my sins and cleanse me from all unrighteousness.

I believe that You died for me on the cross and that You rose again.

Come now, Lord Jesus, and live Your life in me.

Fill me, Lord, with Your Holy Spirit.

Thank You, Lord, for saving me.

In Jesus' name I pray. Amen.

CHAPTER FOUR

WINNING THROUGH OBEDIENCE

Obedience is better than sacrifice, and submission is better than offering the fat of rams.

I SAMUEL 15:22 (NLT)

I can remember when my parents—Thomas Bob Ross and Mary Anna Ross—scanned their eyes across the sanctuary like a radar during worship service at United Baptist Church in Gobler, Missouri. All they had to do was to give us "the look" and we immediately aligned ourselves with the proper behavioral posture. As children, we realized the consequences of inappropriate behavior, whether in public or at home. As our family grew to fourteen children, we were never out of my parents' scope of discipline. They knew exactly what each one of us was doing. Obeying our parents was a form of submission to their authority.

Likewise, God our Heavenly Father wants and expects

that same kind of response to His authority. We know when our actions displease God. The Holy Spirit who is inside us nudges us and reminds us of what the Word of God says; the Holy Spirit leads us into all truth—John 16:13 (KJV). As children of God, we should strive to walk in obedience. Obedience means to comply with the word of God and to do as God's word says. We have to remember that we are citizens of God's Kingdom, and citizens are expected to obey the precepts of that particular government or kingdom. The Bible is our constitution, with explicit guidelines as to how we are to navigate our lives. If we are genuinely in this Christian race to be victorious, we must obey the voice of God.

In teaching us how to pray, Jesus prays these words in Matthew 6:10 (KJV): "Thy Kingdom come. Thy will be done, in earth, as it is in heaven." These are words of obedience. When we invite Jesus into our hearts, His Kingdom comes inside us. With His Kingdom, we should strive to do His will here on earth as it is done in heaven. There is a life principle that propels us to adhere to the will of God, and that principle is "commitment." When we learn to execute commitment in our lives, the life principle will transcend to all areas of our lives. Commitment means to bind ourselves to a task that we have promised to complete, and to remain dedicated to that task. In talking to employers and pastors, commitment is lacking from a great number of people. For the most part, many individuals have become desensitized to keeping their promise, because they know they can justify their absence with an excuse. Excuses nullify our commitments and they are enemies of our commitment. It is a sad commentary when we cannot give our word and stand on it. A life of commitment is a life of success. Proverbs 16:3 says that when we commit to the Lord whatever we do, our plans will succeed.

The Apostle Paul says in Acts 20:24 (KJV): "But none of these things move me, neither count I my life dear unto myself, so that I might finish my course with joy, and the ministry, which I have received of the Lord Jesus, to testify the Gospel of the grace of God."

Our attitude should mirror that of the Apostle Paul; we should strive to complete the task that God has given us and the tasks that we have promised God that we would complete. When we keep our commitment, it transforms our promise into reality. Commitments are known by the actions they prompt—just like love, it is an action word. We must determine in our minds and hearts that we will stick to the tasks that we have promised to complete. Our stewardship is demonstrated when we exercise steadfast commitment and dedication. God wants us to be good stewards of our time, talents, and treasures. Faithfulness is what God requires.

Commitment involves not only showing up for one's appointments or engagements—it means showing up on time. Perpetual tardiness is a poor testimony to committed Christian living. Many people who make tardiness a practice justify it by having the mindset of: "They'd better be glad that I'm here." I have a response to that statement: "There is going to come a time when there is no more time." Jesus says in John 9:4 (KJV), "I must work the works of Him that sent Me, while it is day: the night cometh, when no man can work." While we have the time, let's do the best we can for our Lord, and let's do it with excellence.

The word "day" refers to present opportunities; we must work while we have the chance. The word "night" refers to the time of lost opportunity. When night comes, no one can work. There is going to come a time when there is no more time to do anything. Therefore, we must do the work that God has called us to do, without making any excuses.

Jesus gives an example of a man who made an excuse why he could not follow Him. Matthew 8:21–22 (NIV) says: "Another disciple said to Him, 'Lord, first let me go and bury my father.' But Jesus told him, 'Follow Me, and let the dead bury their own dead.'"

Jesus is not being insensitive in the above passage. He recognized that the man was making excuses why he could not follow Him. In the first place, if the man had to go and bury his father, why would he be roaming about in the crowd when he had a funeral to attend? Biblical scholars question whether the man's father was still living and he was just waiting for him to die. Whatever the case, Jesus knew the man's heart. He knew he was making excuses. When Jesus said "let the dead bury their own dead," He meant "let the spiritually dead bury the physically dead." The man who is making the excuses was obviously spiritually dead. What does this say about us? Are we spiritually dead when we make a lot of excuses why we can't serve the Lord? Think about it!

The following Scripture is a good basis for our practice of a committed life. I Corinthians 15:58 (KJV) says: "Therefore, my beloved brethren, be ye steadfast, unmovable, always abounding in the work of the Lord, forasmuch as ye know that your labor is not in vain in the Lord." These words summarize how we should live a committed life.

Anything worth having is worth the fight. Commitment to the will of God comes with a price. Jesus says in Luke 9:23 (NIV): "If anyone would come after Me, he must deny himself and take up his cross daily and follow Me."

As Christians, we need to ask ourselves if we pay the full price of what is required to sincerely come after Jesus.

The first step is to *deny ourselves*. When we deny ourselves we renounce the selfish desires of the flesh. The flesh rules our lives until we dethrone the longing of our carnal nature. After dethroning the flesh, we must put Jesus on the throne of our hearts and allow Him to make each move in our lives. Many times we say that we present ourselves to God as a living sacrifice. But the thing about living sacrifices is that they tend to keep getting off the altar. Let's stay on the altar and remain slaughtered before our Lord.

Jesus says in Luke 14:33 (KJV), "So likewise, whosoever he be of you that forsaketh not all that he hath, he cannot be My disciple." We are stewards in this life. Nothing belongs to us. When we surrender our will to Jesus, we give Him everything else that we own. Our life is not our own.

I remember when both our sons were born—Charlie Jr. and Andrew. I personally gave them to the Lord in the hospital room. They are more than three years apart in birth order. After each birth, I prayed a prayer of thanksgiving and said, "Lord, I give this child back to You. Use him as You will. Give my husband, Charles, and I the wisdom to raise Your child properly." Our boys are now young men, and I still pray for them daily and ask God to bless them and keep them in His care.

Just like we let go of our children, we must let go of our own lives. Jesus says in Luke 9:24 (NIV): "For whoever wants to save his life will lose it, but whoever loses his life for Me will save it." We must throw our hands up in the air and say, "Lord, I am Yours." Our words must be words of action. When we unswervingly give our hearts to Jesus, we will gain eternal life. That's what Jesus meant in the above Scripture when He said that "whoever loses his life for Me will save it."

Another way we pay the price in commitment is by *taking up our cross daily.* A cross is an instrument of death—a symbol of suffering and shame. In biblical times, a person was hung on a cross for committing the most hideous crime. Jesus committed no crime. He loved us so much that

He paid the price for us by dying for our sins. Jesus says in Luke 14:27 that anyone who does not carry his cross and follow Him cannot be His disciple. If we don't bear the cross of suffering that besets us each day, then we cannot be a follower and student of Jesus. Jesus says the following in Matthew 11:29 (NIV): "Take My yoke upon you and learn from Me, for I am gentle and humble in heart, and you will find rest for your souls."

A disciple is a student and a follower of Jesus; Jesus exhorts us to learn from Him. When we give Jesus all of our cares or cast our cares upon Jesus, He will bear our burdens and give us His rest and peace. Jesus says in Matthew 10:38 (KJV) that anyone who does not take his cross and follow Him is not worthy of Him. In other words, we are not deserving of Jesus if we do not bear our cross of suffering. Suffering enables us to conform to the image of Jesus. Hebrews 5:8 (KJV) says that Jesus learned obedience from the things He suffered. From suffering, Jesus learned to say to our heavenly Father, "Not My will but Your will be done."

A final way from our text to pay the price for commitment is to *follow Jesus.* The word "follow" means to come after or to go after. Jesus says in Matthew 4:19–20 (NIV): "Come, follow Me, and I will make you fishers of men." At once the disciples left their nets and followed Him. Jesus's disciples were fishing along the shore of the Sea of Galilee when He called them. They exercised prompt obedience and followed Him. Jesus makes us fishers of men when we obey Him; He gives us the wisdom, power, and venues to evangelize. All we have to say is "Yes, Lord, I will follow You wherever You lead me."

A tangible example of denying ourselves, taking up our cross daily and following Jesus can be demonstrated by taking a blank piece of paper and writing our name at the very bottom. Then, we can give this piece of paper to God, and say, "Lord, on this blank piece of paper with my name at the bottom, please write whatever You will, and I will do it. I am Yours." Can we do this exercise and mean it? Our signature at the bottom of this paper indicates that our surrender is binding. Such as exercise is an exercise of commitment.

WHAT'S LOVE GOT TO DO WITH OBEDIENCE?

What does love have to do with winning through obedience? Everything! Jesus says in John 14:15 (KJV) that if we love Him we will obey His commands. It was not easy for Jesus to give up the comforts of heaven and descend to the discomforts of earth. He did it out of love and obedience to the Father. Jesus surrendered His will to the will of the Father—this is why He could say, "Thy will be done."

Another Scripture verse that infers that love and obedience must co-exist is found in II John 1:6 (KJV). It says: "And this is love, that we walk after His commandments. This is the commandment, That, as ye have heard from the beginning, ye should walk in it." True love is exemplified by a lifestyle of obedience. Love is known by the actions that it prompts. We are able to love because of the agape love that we possess. Agape love defines the nature of God. God is love; therefore, His love abides in us as His children. Our only recourse is to walk in love in our daily encounters, since the love of God is flowing in our hearts. Since we love God, we will obey Him.

There was a children's Sunday school class discussing love. The teacher called on young Ben, a six-year-old boy, to give her a definition of love. Ben said, "Love is when my mommy reads me a bedtime story every night. But real love is when she doesn't skip any pages."

God views real love in the same manner. When we truly

love God, we won't take any short cuts in attempts to make things more convenient for us. We will follow the entire dictates of God's command.

Love is defined in I Corinthians 13:4–5 (NLT) as being "patient, kind, not jealous or boastful or proud or rude. It does not demand its own way. It is not irritable, and it keeps no record of being wronged." True love can be measured by the guidelines of this definition. A good demonstration of this definition is stated in Romans 5:8 (NKJV), which says: "But God demonstrates His own love toward us, in that while we were still sinners, Christ died for us." There were no conditions for God's love for us; even if there had been, we could not have manufactured the kind of behavior that would have been required to earn Christ's dying for us on the cross. Love is unconditional and volitional—a matter of the will. Love is a matter of grace, which is God's unearned favor.

We have seen God's love demonstrated for us. What must we do to demonstrate our love for God? Jesus explains this in His conversation with an expert of the law as He answers his question regarding what was the greatest of all of the commandments. Jesus replied in Matthew 22:37–40 (NIV), "'Love the Lord your God with all your heart, and with all your soul, and with all your mind.' This is the first and greatest commandment. And the second is like it: 'Love your neighbor as yourself.' All the Law and the Prophets hang on these two commandments."

If we love God with all of our being, and love our neighbors as ourselves, we will keep all of the other commandments. These two commandments will guide our demonstration of love toward God, others, and ourselves.

I John 4:20 (NIV) states that "if anyone says, 'I love God,' yet hates his brother, he is a liar. For anyone who does not love his brother, whom he has seen, cannot love God, whom he has not seen." The key is to fall in love with

God—then we can love our brother. Love is of God and will be manifested by how we treat those who we see every day.

There was a family who moved from one part of town to another. The distance was about a thirty-minute drive. The two children loved attending Sunday school at their previous location, and they asked their dad if he could continue to transport them to this particular Sunday school. The dad responded, "There are plenty of good Sunday Schools in this neighborhood, and I don't see why I have to drive you clear across town." The two children—nine-year-old Jason and six-year-old Sarah—replied, "Yeah, Dad, but do they know how to love a fellow over there?" Love is known by the actions it prompts. Children are the best judge for the presence of genuine love.

In assessing what love has to do with obedience, we witness that real love remains. This is demonstrated in the story of Ruth, in which Ruth, whose name means "friendship," showed unrelenting love and devotion to her mother-in-law, Naomi. Naomi and her husband, Elimelech, left Bethlehem due to famine, and moved to Moab to secure a better living for their family. Their two sons, Mahlon and Kilion, accompanied them. Soon after their relocation, Naomi's husband, Elimelech, died. The two sons then married two Moabite women: Mahlon married Ruth, and Kilion married Orpah. After ten years, their husbands died, leaving Naomi, Ruth, and Orpah as three destitute widows. In Ruth 1:12–13 (NIV), Naomi attempted to persuade her daughters-in-law to return home to their families in Moab: "Return home, my daughters; I am too old to have another husband. Even if I thought there was still hope for me—even if I had a husband tonight and then gave birth to sons—would you wait until they grew up? Would you remain unmarried for them? No, my daughters. It is more bitter for me than for you, because the Lord's hand has gone out against me!"

Naomi felt like her spiritual tank was on "E." She felt empty in every way—even her womb felt empty. She thought that the Lord's hand had gone out against her. We know this wasn't true, but there are times when we feel the same way. God has promised never to leave or forsake us (Hebrews 13:5b KJV). Nevertheless, there are times when all things point in the opposite direction. We have all heard the expression, "When it rains, it pours." Of course, this is not a Biblical statement. Negative statements are all lies from the devil. God is always fighting for us. Our situations are not always what they appear to be. Therefore, we walk by faith and not by sight. In the story of Ruth, God sets the stage for more blessings than Naomi or Ruth could have ever imagined.

Naomi continued to urge Ruth to go back to her family after Orpah made the decision to return to her family. Ruth 1:14–16 (NIV) says: "At this, they wept again. Then Orpah kissed her mother-in-law good-bye, but Ruth clung to her. 'Look,' said Naomi, 'your sister-in-law is going back to her people and her gods. Go back with her.' But Ruth replied, 'Don't urge me to leave you or to turn back from you. Where you go I will go, and where you stay I will stay. Your people will be my people and your God my God.'"

We witness enormous loyalty, love, and devotion from Ruth toward her mother-in-law, Naomi. Coming from a Gentile background, Ruth had wholeheartedly chosen the God of Israel, and of her own volition was willing to adopt the Jewish way of life. In Ruth 1:17 (NIV), she made an oath by saying: "Where you die I will die, and there I will be buried. May the Lord deal with me, be it ever so severely, if anything but death separates you and me." This is an oath statement in the name of Israel's God, which is a true display of commitment.

The Bible says in Ruth 1:18 that when Naomi realized that Ruth was determined to go with her, she stopped urging her. Ruth was determined, which was a matter of her will. As a result of Ruth's unselfish love for Naomi, Boaz, a wealthy kinsman-redeemer, took notice of her. (A "kinsman-redeemer" was a relative who was responsible for protecting the interests of members of the extended family.) Since Boaz was related to Ruth's former husband, Mahlon, and since he was the closest male relative, he was responsible for protecting Ruth and marrying her. Boaz said the following in Ruth 2:11–12 (NIV): "I've been told all about what you have done for your mother-in-law since the death of your husband—how you left your father and mother and your homeland and came to live with a people you did not know before. May the Lord repay you for what you have done. May you be richly rewarded by the Lord, the God of Israel, under whose wings you have come to take refuge."

Ruth was tremendously rewarded by God for her profound love and commitment to her mother-in-law, Naomi. Over time, Ruth and Boaz got married and had a son. Ruth 1:17 says that they named their son Obed. He became the father of Jesse, who was the father of King David. What we make happen for others, God will make happen for us. Ruth was rewarded for her kindness. She began as a Moabite woman who was left a widow. Now she is in the direct lineage of Jesus. Naomi remarked that Ruth was better to her than seven sons. The number seven is the number for perfection. Naomi now had a grandson who could fill her emptiness and loneliness. God has promised to bless us if we don't give up. Naomi had graduated from being empty to being completely full—actually, to being overflowing. Her name was no longer "Mara," which means "bitter." She became happy and renewed. Ruth 4:15 says that Obed would renew her life and sustain her in her old age. We serve a wonderful God. Naomi never could have imagined that God would bless her to this magnitude. God is no respecter of persons; He has no favorites. What He did for Naomi and Ruth, He will do for you! In your loneliness, encourage someone else. What you make happen for others, God will make happen for you.

Galatians 6:9 (KJV) says, "And let us not be weary in well doing: for in due season we shall reap, if we faint not." Remember to hang in there. Never give up. Whenever you feel like your spiritual thermometer is running on low, pour yourself into the life of someone else and happiness will begin to elevate in your life. When we sow joy, we reap joy in return. Let's get our focus off of ourselves and redirect our attention to others. We will be amazed by how rapidly God turns things around in our lives.

LED BY THE HOLY SPIRIT

Winning through obedience entails being led by the Holy Spirit of God. Since Jesus was led by the Holy Spirit during His earthly ministry, how much more should we be led by the Holy Spirit. Jesus said in John 10:27 (NKJV): "My sheep hear My voice, and I know them, and they follow Me." Jesus knows us and we know Him because of our relationship with Him. Since we have a relationship with Him, we will know His voice and follow Him. Whenever my husband, Charles, calls me on the phone, I don't have to say, "Who is this?" I already know, because, after many years of marriage, I know his voice and he knows mine. This concept is true for my sons, our family, friends, and members of the congregation. I recognize their voices the moment they say, "Hello."

The Holy Spirit lives inside us, guiding us into truth. We will know the voice of Jesus because of the leading of the Holy Spirit. Jesus said in John 16:13 (KJV): "Howbeit when He, the Spirit of truth, is come, He will guide you into all truth: for He shall not speak of Himself; but whatsoever He shall hear, that shall He speak: and He will show you things to come." The Holy Spirit is the third person of the Trinity, and Jesus had to go away before He could come. Now that the Holy Spirit is here among us, He dwells in every believer, leading us into all righteousness and all truth. He will say whatever God the Father tells Him to say.

I read a story about a little girl and her father, who were walking through the woods. It was a muddy day, and the little girl looked up at her father and said, "Daddy, I want to walk in your exact steps so that if you don't get mud on your shoes then I won't get mud on my shoes." That is the way we should feel about the Spirit of truth; He will lead us into all truth, and we don't have to worry about getting the mud of the world on our feet.

I have a friend who is a caregiver for her elderly mother. My friend was running errands when the Holy Spirit spoke to her very profoundly and said, "Go home now!" She knew it was the voice of the Holy Spirit and she drove home as quickly as she could. When she arrived, she found a pot on the stove at the point of combustion. All of the water had boiled out of the pot and it was at the point of exploding into flames. My friend immediately grabbed the glowing red pot and put it into the kitchen sink. If she had arrived a few seconds later, the house would have been engulfed in flames. Her elderly mother awakened just as she entered the door, totally oblivious to what had occurred and grossly unaware of her imminent danger. My friend's eighty-four-year-old mother did not realize that her deep sleep had overtaken her. She promised never to cook again without someone being present in the home.

My friend has since shared this Spirit-led experience with prayer groups in her church and others in her sphere of influence. The voice of the Holy Spirit is prolific and profound. As children of God, we need to follow the leading of the Holy Spirit. Romans 8:14 (KJV) says: "For as many as are led by the Spirit of God, they are the sons of God." God created everyone, but not everyone is a child of God. We must be born into His family. Once we are born into His family by inviting Jesus into our hearts, we can say, "Abba, Father"—which means "Daddy God." As sons and daughters of God, we have His DNA inside us. This means that we were created in the image of God, and we must live to represent His character. Our daily lives must exemplify the nature of God. We can only do this with the leading of the Holy Spirit.

The Holy Spirit guides us so that we won't follow the temptations of Satan. We must not be deceived. Just because we are Christians does not mean that the devil is not on our trail. The devil's mission is to prevent us from fulfilling our mission of advancing the Kingdom of God and making heaven our home. We can resist the temptation of Satan the very same way that Jesus resisted temptations and overcame the devil.

In observing the three temptations of Jesus in the wilderness, we will recognize that Jesus remained faithful throughout those encounters and that He is a model for all believers when we are tempted. The temptations started right after Jesus was baptized by John the Baptist and He was led into the wilderness by the Holy Spirit to be tempted by the devil. God authenticated His Son at His baptism and He expressed His support for Jesus His Son.

Matthew 3:16–17 (NIV) says: "As soon as Jesus was baptized, He went up out of the water. At that moment heaven was opened, and He saw the Spirit of God descending like a dove and lighting on Him. And a voice from heaven said, 'This is My Son, whom I love; with Him I am well pleased.'" Jesus began His earthly ministry after His baptism. The Holy Spirit came down upon Him and dwelled inside of Him in order to equip Him for the work of the ministry. Although Jesus was fully God and fully man, He needed the empowering of the Holy Spirit for the human realm, and He wanted to be an example for us.

Matthew 4:1–2 (NIV) says: "Then Jesus was led by the Spirit into the desert to be tempted by the devil. After fasting forty days and forty nights, He was hungry." The devil tempts us at our point of craving or physical need. The word "temptation" means "to be enticed." The devil tempts us to do evil or wrong. Being tempted by Satan is not a sin; yielding to temptation is a sin. God tests us to prove what is on the inside of our hearts. God does not tempt us. He is a loving God who wants His children to succeed for His glory. Jesus had fasted for forty days and forty nights; therefore, He was hungry and the devil took advantage of His physical hunger. The number forty symbolizes a period of testing, trial, or probation. Jesus passed His test. The children of Israel who were tested in the wilderness for forty years did not pass theirs. Deuteronomy 8:2 (NIV) says: "Remember how the Lord your God led you all the way in the desert these forty years, to humble you and to test you in order to know what was in your heart, whether or not you would keep His commands."

When Jesus was tempted by the devil, He always quoted Scripture. This is an example to us of how we need to respond to Satan when we are tempted to do evil or wrong. Matthew 4:3–4 (NIV) says: "The tempter came to Him and said, 'If you are the Son of God, tell these stones to become bread.' Jesus answered, 'It is written: "Man does not live on bread alone, but on every word that comes from the mouth of God."'" The devil is like a big bully trying to challenge Jesus to doubt His identity and trying to entice Jesus to use His supernatural power to satisfy His own physical need. It is clear that Jesus looks to God the Father to meet all of His needs. When Jesus says, "It is written: 'Man does not live on bread alone but on every word that comes from the mouth of God,'" this Scripture is taken from Deuteronomy 8:3.

In the second temptation, the devil tried to entice Jesus to attract public attention. Matthew 4:5–6 (NIV) says: "Then the devil took Him to the Holy City and had Him stand on the highest point of the temple. 'If you are the Son of God,' he said, 'throw Yourself down. For it is written: "He will command His angels concerning you and they will lift you up in their hands, so that you will not strike Your foot against a stone."'" In quoting Psalm 91:11–12, the devil misrepresented it. The original chapter focuses on the refuge of God and dwelling in the secret place of God. The devil twisted it to tempt Jesus to test God. Jesus responded by quoting Deuteronomy 6:16: "It is also written: 'Do not put the Lord your God to the test'" (Matthew 4:7 NIV). God is Supreme and it is a sin to try to put Him to the test. Doing so is an act of pride, and pride is sin before our holy God. Remember, pride is the reason Satan was kicked out of heaven in the first place (Isaiah 14:12–14).

In the third temptation, the devil took Jesus to another high place. Matthew 4:8–9 (NIV) says: "Again, the devil took Him to a very high mountain and showed Him all the kingdoms of the world and their splendor. 'All this I will give You,' he said, 'if you will bow down and worship me.'"

Matthew 4:10 (NIV) says: "Jesus said to him, 'Away from Me, Satan! For it is written: "Worship the Lord your God, and serve Him only.'" Jesus quoted Deuteronomy 6:13. When faced with temptation from Satan, we need to do precisely what Jesus did. We need to say, "It is written . . ." and respond with the Word of God. It is paramount that we know the Word of God so that we can quote Scripture in the appropriate situation.

The devil will leave us for a season and return. Matthew 4:11 (NIV) says: "Then the devil left Him, and angels came and attended Him." The angels came and ministered to Jesus and met His every need. We must depend on Jesus at all times. He will send His angels to care for our needs.

An important Scripture to know is James 4:7–8 (KJV). It reads as follows: "Submit yourselves therefore to God. Resist the devil, and he will flee from you. Draw nigh to God, and He will draw nigh to you."

Whenever we draw near to God, He will draw near to you. Being led by the Holy Spirit involves drawing near to God at all times. During those wilderness experiences, God is with us. The trials will only make us stronger and they will prove what is really in our hearts. The devil tempts us to serve him and not God. The devil's objective is for us to perish in Hell with him and his demons. God's objective is for us to have everlasting life in heaven with Him and Jesus.

John 3:16 (NKJV) says: "For God so loved the world that He gave His only begotten Son, that whoever believes in Him should not perish but have everlasting life."

God's mission is for all of us to have everlasting life. He gave us His Holy Spirit to lead us into all truth.

OBEDIENCE IN THE VALLEY

We are all going to have valley experiences; nevertheless, we must exercise obedience at all costs. A "valley experience" is when you are in a low place in your life, or a state of depression. Some of the causes of valley experiences are:

- Trauma or distress
- Grief—the loss of loved ones
- Family problems
- Financial troubles
- Unemployment
- Serious illness
- Personal problems

Any of the problems above can cause one to enter into a state of hopelessness. Despite how we feel, we must obey the word of God. God tells us to speak His word during troubled times. His word has creative abilities. During creation in the book of Genesis, God said, "Let there be . . ." and creation occurred. Our words are powerful and active; therefore, we must employ them.

In Psalm 23:4 (NKJV) David says, "Yea, thou I walk through the valley of the shadow of death, I will fear no evil; for You are with me; Your rod and Your staff, they comfort me." Many of us have memorized this passage. As we encounter valley experiences, God is with us. He is our Shepherd and His rod and staff reassures. The rod and staff are both instruments of authority. The rod was used by the shepherd for counting, guiding, rescuing, and protecting the sheep. The staff was used for support of the shepherd and rescuing the sheep. Metaphorically, God's presence provides these qualities for us. He will always be with us to care for us in whatever manner we need Him. It is detrimental for us to abide in fear because fear is the opposite of faith. When we are genuinely aware of God's presence, fear will vanish.

God's word tells us in II Timothy 1:7 (NKJV), "For God

has not given us a spirit of fear, but of power and of love and of a sound mind." Fear is not of God; it is from the devil and it cancels out our faith. Fear paralyzes us and renders us helpless. When confronted with fear, we must grab hold of our power, love, and sound mind—all tools of the Holy Spirit.

In the story of the valley of dry bones in Ezekiel, we learn that the bones are symbolic of hopelessness, death, and emptiness. The house of Israel experienced dryness because they had been taken into exile by the Babylonians. We learn in this passage that God commanded Ezekiel, a prophet, to prophesy to the dry bones. The word "prophesy" means "to forth-tell God's word and to foretell God's word." When we forth-tell God's word, we speak forth His promises; when we foretell God's word, we speak it before it happens. Romans 4:17 (KJV) says, "(As it is written, I have made thee a father of many nations,) before him whom he believed, even God, who quickeneth the dead, and calleth those things which be not as though they were."

God is speaking about Abraham, who was considered the father of the Jews and believing Gentiles; this is why he is called "a father of many nations." Abraham and Sarah were past the age of childbearing when their son Isaac was born—Abraham was one hundred and Sarah was ninety. Through Isaac's birth, God demonstrated His ability to create something out of an impossible situation. If we are going to be victorious in this Christian journey, we must trust God for the impossible. We must believe that nothing is impossible with God!

God has given us creative ability with our tongues. We can literally speak life to dead situations. I am reminded of a plant that my mother-in-law, Lula Blakley, who is now deceased, possessed in her home. The plant appeared to be dead. She kept watering it. After a few weeks, the plant was flourishing and healthy. God's word works in a similar fashion. We can water dead situations with the word of God and life will re-appear.

Ezekiel 37:1–4 (NIV) speaks of the valley of dry bones. It reads: "The hand of the Lord was upon me, and He brought me out by the Spirit of the Lord and set me in the middle of a valley; it was full of bones. He led me back and forth among them, and I saw a great many bones on the floor of the valley, bones that were very dry. He asked me, 'Son of man, can these bones live?' I said, 'O Sovereign Lord, You alone know.' Then He said to me, 'Prophesy to these bones and say to them, "Dry bones hear the word of the Lord!"'"

God ordered Ezekiel in a vision to speak to the dry bones, and commanded them to hear the promises that He was about to deliver. Ezekiel knew that these bones had no sign of life—and yet, God was commanding them to live.

Ezekiel 37:5–6 says (NIV) says: "This is what the Sovereign Lord says to these bones: 'I will make breath enter you, and you will come to life. I will attach tendons to you and make flesh come upon you and cover you with skin; I will put breath in you, and you will come to life. Then you will know that I am the Lord.'"

The Lord commanded Ezekiel to prophesy to these dead bones so that they would reconnect and come to life again. This vision is indicative of the House of Israel. God was going to bring them out of Babylonian exile and put new life in them. The new life was the Holy Spirit. Israel would come to life again and be restored to their homeland. A dead nation would be totally restored because breath entered them. The Hebrew word for breath is "ruach." This word also means wind, air, strength, or Holy Spirit. When breath or new life was returned to dead Israel, they would know that God was the Lord. The same principle is applicable to us modern-day Christians. When God totally transforms our lives by the power of the Holy Spirit, we should know that no human effort did this miraculous feat. Only the hand of God can make us full of life. When this occurs, we will know that He is the Lord God Almighty!

If you don't know the Lord as your personal Savior, you may invite Him into your heart by praying the following prayer:

THE SINNER'S PRAYER

Lord, Jesus, I am a sinner.

Please forgive me of all my sins and cleanse me from all unrighteousness.

I believe that You died for me on the cross and that You rose again.

Come now, Lord Jesus, and live Your life in me.

Fill me, Lord, with Your Holy Spirit.

Thank You, Lord, for saving me.

In Jesus' name I pray. Amen.

If you just prayed this prayer for the first time, you are born again. Make plans now to contact your pastor or ministry leader and inform them of your decision. You need to be baptized and live a life for Jesus! Congratulations on this new chapter in your life, as a new creation in Christ Jesus!

CHAPTER FIVE

WINNING THROUGH THE CROSS

They overcame him by the blood of the Lamb and by the word of their testimony.

REVELATIONS 12:11 (NIV)

The blood of Jesus is the key to victorious Christian living and to winning in every round or season of our lives. The blood of Jesus enables us to win over sin and death. Have you ever given blood at the hospital or blood bank? When you gave blood in that setting, you did not have to give your life. When Jesus gave blood, He gave His life, shedding His blood at Calvary for our sins. Jesus said in John 10:10b (KJV), "I am come that they might have life, and that they might have it more abundantly."

The cross is an emblem of suffering and shame, and it is symbolic of life because Jesus sacrificed His life on the cross in order that we may have eternal life. Hebrews 9:22

(KJV) says: "And almost all things are by the law purged with blood; and without shedding of blood is no remission." We can be certain that our sins are forgiven when we invite Jesus into our hearts and ask Him to forgive us our sins. When we take this step, He will cleanse us from all unrighteousness. Even when we sin after this point, all we have to do is confess our sins and repent, and we will be forgiven by our Master. The blood of Jesus frees us from our sins. Revelation 1:5b (KJV) says, "Unto Him that loved us, and washed us from our sins in His own blood."

We should make every attempt to flee from sin. It has been said that "Sin will take you farther than you want to go. You will stay longer than you want to stay, and you will pay more than you want to pay." This adage is true. There are consequences for our sins—sure, we will be forgiven, but we have to pay the price. The devil intensifies his strategies to lure us into sin the more we grow in our relationship with Jesus. Nevertheless, Jesus has not left us helpless. Revelation 12:11 (NIV) says: "They overcame him by the blood of the Lamb and by the word of their testimony." We can overcome the attacks of Satan by applying the blood of Jesus to the situation. I plead the blood of Jesus over negative thoughts or circumstances. I plead the blood of Jesus over my family and ministry because there is wonder-working power in the blood. We can also overcome Satan by the word of our testimony. We can speak the word of God to negative or challenging situations. We can even call things that are not as though they were (Romans 4:17b).

A member of our church had to get a physical when she applied for a job. She was nervous that her blood pressure was elevated. She prayed, "Lord, you know that I need this job. So blood pressure, I command you to go down. I command you, blood pressure, to drop down to normal range." She said the Holy Spirit spoke to her and told her to go get a drink of water; she did. After that, she asked the person in charge to retake her blood pressure. When her blood pressure was retaken, it was down to normal range. She got the job that she so desperately needed. Praise God! Nothing is too hard for our God.

THE BLOOD OF JESUS GIVES ATONEMENT

Leviticus 17:11 (NIV) says: "For the life of a creature is in the blood. And I have given it to you to make atonement for yourselves on the altar; it is the blood that makes atonement for one's life." In the Old Testament, it was forbidden for the Israelites to consume blood. When they went hunting, they had to drain the blood out of the animal before eating it. Those who consumed blood were to be cut off from the camp. Blood symbolized life, and life was to be treated with respect. God gave the blood to His people to make atonement on the altar for their sins—an altar is a place of sacrifice. In the Old Covenant, the priest would sacrifice a bull, goat, lamb, or some other animal on the altar for the sins of the people. The sacrifice had to be without blemish and without defect.

According to *Vine's Concise Dictionary of Bible Words,* the word "atone," which comes from the Hebrew word "kapar," means:

- To cover over
- To make amends
- To pacify God's wrath
- To appease God

In the New Covenant, Jesus was the perfect sacrifice to atone for the sins of the people. Hebrews 2:17 (NIV) says: "For this reason, He had to be made like His brothers in every way, in order that He might become a merciful and faithful high priest in service to God, and that He might make atonement for the sins of the people." Jesus died in our place, meaning that He was our substitute. In order for Jesus to be the perfect sacrifice for the sins of the people, He had to be like us but without sin. He was the perfect lamb—without blemish and without defect. Only Jesus Christ could be our merciful and faithful High Priest, making atonement for our sins.

THE BLOOD OF JESUS GIVES JUSTIFICATION

It is good to know that we can be justified because of the blood of Jesus. We are truly guilty of sin because of the sin committed by Adam and Eve in the Garden. Their sin transferred to all humanity. Glory be to God, who gave us a way to escape eternal damnation. Although we are sinners, we are justified by the blood of Jesus.

Justification means to be made right through the blood of Jesus Christ. Our righteousness is through Jesus Christ. Romans 5:9 (KJV) says: "Much more then, being now justified by His blood, we shall be saved from wrath through Him." Justification is a means of appeasing God's righteous wrath. The blood of Jesus makes us right with God the Father.

Romans 3:23–24 (KJV) says: "For all have sinned, and come short of the glory of God; being justified freely by His grace through the redemption that is in Christ Jesus." If we say that we have never sinned, we are liars. We all have sinned, and we are saved by grace that has been freely given to us by Jesus Christ.

THE BLOOD OF JESUS GIVES RECONCILIATION

Have you ever fallen out of relationship with someone? It

can cause a sense of total isolation, rejection, and abandonment. Imagine falling out of relationship with Jesus and God the Father. This situation would be devastating! However, this was our state before Jesus died for us on the cross. Since Jesus shed His blood for us, we can now have eternal life. When Jesus comes into our hearts, we too will be brought back into relationship with God the Father. The word "reconciliation" means to change from being an enemy to being a friend. It means to restore relationship.

Because of reconciliation, I am a friend of Jesus and you can be also. To know Jesus is to be in relationship with Him. II Corinthians 5:17–18 (KJV) says: "Therefore if any man be in Christ, he is a new creature: old things are passed away; behold, all things are become new. And all things are of God, who hath reconciled us to Himself by Jesus Christ, and hath given to us the ministry of reconciliation." All of us as Christians have been given this ministry of reconciliation. Our calling or assignment is to spread the Gospel so that others will come into relationship with God Almighty. The only thing we can take to heaven with us is another soul.

II Corinthians 5:19 (KJV) says: "To wit, that God was in Christ, reconciling the world unto Himself, not imputing their trespasses unto them; and hath committed unto us the word of reconciliation." We have a mandate to spread this message of reconciliation. We have a part in building the Kingdom of God by bringing others into relationship with Jesus and God the Father. This assignment makes us ambassadors. II Corinthians 5:20 (KJV) says: "Now then we are ambassadors for Christ, as though God did beseech you by us: we pray you in Christ's stead, be ye reconciled to God."

An ambassador is a representative in residence. We are in this world but not of it. Therefore, we are in residence in this world, representing our God in our speech and action. The only Jesus some people will see is in each of us Christians.

Let's make it our mandate to tell others about Jesus and about the power in His precious blood. The blood of Jesus has the power to save us from sin and to totally transform our lives. I read a story about a little boy—about seven years old—who was told that he could save his sister's life by giving her some of his blood in a blood transfusion. He did not really understand the full terms of this proposition. He was told that his sister was dying and that he was the only one who had her rare blood type. So he agreed to give her some of his blood if it would save her life. When he made this decision, his bottom lip began to tremble and his hands began to shake. He was fearful; nevertheless, he was bold in making this decision. The time arrived for the young boy to give his sister some of his blood, and he did it gallantly. Toward the end of the ordeal, he looked up at the doctor and said, "Doctor, when do I die?" The doctor realized at that point that the young boy had been so fearful because he thought he was giving his life for his sister. It was at this moment that the boy realized that he could give blood to his sister and yet save his own life.

A blood transfusion is immensely different from a blood transformation. When Jesus died for us on the cross, He gave us an opportunity to be totally transformed. The huge difference is that Jesus had to die. It was not a mere blood transfusion in which He would keep His life. He gave His life to save us from our sins by lovingly dying for us on the cross.

EVIDENCE OF THE CROSS

You have probably heard the question asked, "If you were

arrested for being a Christian, would there be enough evidence to convict you?" When you think about that question, do you nod your head and say, "Yes"? When the blood of Jesus is on the doorpost of our hearts, we will exhibit the evidence of the cross. The life-changing power of the blood of Jesus will exude from our lives.

Jesus admonishes us in Matthew 5:16 (NKJV) to let our light shine before men. He says, "Let your light so shine before men, that they may see your good works and glorify your Father in heaven." The word "glorify" means "to praise God our Father." As Christians, we should live in such a manner that others around us should see Jesus. We are the only Bible that some people will ever read. I am reminded of a story that I read years ago, about a carpenter who was also a minister. He was called to do some carpentry work in a nearby neighborhood. As he worked tirelessly, a small girl watched him intently. He was curious about her steadfastness in watching him work, so he asked, "Little girl, are you interested in carpentry work?" She shrugged her shoulders and said, "No." Then he asked, "Well, do you enjoy watching people work?"

She solemnly responded by saying, "No."

With that response, the preacher asked, "Then why do you keep watching me?"

She replied, "I just want to hear what a preacher says when he hits his finger with a hammer."

The words that come out of our mouths are a means of letting our light shine for the whole world to see. This little girl wanted to hear the words that came from a preacher's mouth when he was confronted with pain. Jesus gives another Scripture that deals with showing the evidence that He lives within us. Matthew 7:16–17 (NIV) says, "By their fruit you will recognize them. Do people pick grapes from thorn bushes, or figs from thistles? Likewise every good tree bears good fruit, but a bad tree bears bad fruit."

People are watching our actions and listening to the

words that come from our lips. Do we glorify God in all that we do or say? When the power of the blood of Jesus is operating in our hearts, good fruit will come forth from us. People may pick our good fruit. Nevertheless, if the blood of Jesus is not operating in our hearts, bad fruit will come from us. We cannot hide the truth of who we are on the inside.

Here's a definition of the word "evidence":

- Comes from the Greek word, *eleg'chos*
- Proof or visible sign of something
- Used to persuade or convince
- Reveals truth; it is obvious

The real evidence of the power of the blood of Jesus operating in our lives is recognized by our love walk. Jesus says in John 13:35 (NLT): "Your love for one another will prove to the world that you are My disciples." We don't have to have a bumper sticker on our cars or wear a sign on our backs that says "love." Our love for one another will reveal that we are followers of Jesus Christ. Love is known by the actions it prompts. We are most like Jesus and God the Father when we love one another. The Bible says in I John 4:8 (KJV) that God is love.

I am reminded of the life of Saul before he became Apostle Paul. His life was not characteristic of the love of Jesus. He had to be converted; he had to change from a life of persecuting Christians to a life of promoting Jesus and preaching His word. Saul underwent three phases or transitions in his conversion process. The first one was a change from maliciousness. The word "malicious" means "inflicting harm or suffering upon another."

CHANGE OF MALICIOUSNESS

In the next few Scriptures, we see how malicious Saul

was in persecuting the Christians. Acts 8:2–3 (NIV) says, "Godly men buried Steven and mourned deeply for him. But Saul began to destroy the church. Going from house to house, he dragged off men and women and put them in prison." Steven had been a devout man of God who was one of the seven leaders of the church. He was full of wisdom and full of the Holy Spirit. Saul authorized the stoning of Steven. He continued to destroy the church and persecute men and women who worshiped Jesus.

Acts 9:1–2 (NIV) says: "Meanwhile, Saul was still breathing out murderous threats against the Lord's disciples. He went to the high priest and asked him for letters to the synagogues in Damascus, so that if he found any there who belonged to the Way, whether men or women, he might take them as prisoners to Jerusalem."

Damascus was 150 miles from Jerusalem and a four- to six-day journey by horse. Saul was willing to make this journey in order to persecute anyone who followed Jesus—following Jesus was known as the Way. In John 14:6 (KJV), Jesus says: "I am the way, the truth, and the life: no man cometh unto the Father, but by Me." Jesus stopped Saul in his tracks when he knocked him off of his horse on the way to Damascus. In this conversion encounter, Saul had a change of mind, which is phase two of this process of changing from persecuting Christians to promoting Jesus.

CHANGE OF MINDSET

Acts 9:3–6 (NIV) says: "As he neared Damascus on his journey, suddenly a light from heaven flashed around him. He fell to the ground and heard a voice say to him, 'Saul, Saul, why do you persecute Me?' 'Who are you, Lord?' Saul asked. 'I am Jesus, whom you are persecuting,' He replied.

'Now get up and go into the city, and you will be told what you must do.'"

Saul had to have a change of mind. The battleground for the devil is the mind. Saul was very educated and highly knowledgeable in the Jewish law. He thought he was right in his zeal to persecute Christians. But the light of Jesus blinded him and he had a change in his thinking. Only the transforming light of Jesus can renew our minds and make us into entirely new people. The Bible says the following in Romans 12:2 (NIV): "Do not conform any longer to the pattern of this world, but be transformed by the renewing of your mind. Then you will be able to test and approve what God's will is—His good, pleasing and perfect will." By knowing God's will, Saul knew that he had a new mission—one of exercising the same zeal but channeling it heavenward in Jesus Christ.

When Jesus addressed Saul by stating his name twice in succession, Saul knew that he was in the presence of God. He didn't quite understand everything that was occurring, but he definitely knew he was in God's presence. The voice of Jesus is transforming and life-changing. Saul was changed instantly. Nevertheless, he remained blind for three days and did not eat until Ananias came and laid hands on him. Saul now had a new mission.

CHANGE OF MISSION

Acts 9:8–12 (NIV) says: "Saul got up from the ground, but when he opened his eyes he could see nothing. So they led him by the hand into Damascus. For three days he was blind, and did not eat or drink anything. In Damascus there was a disciple named Ananias. The lord called to him in a vision, 'Ananias!'

"'Yes, Lord,' he answered. The Lord told him, 'Go to the house of Judas on Straight Street and ask for a man from Tarsus named Saul, for he is praying. In a vision he has seen a man named Ananias come and place his hands on him to restore his sight.'"

When Jesus gave Ananias the task of laying hands on Saul so that he could restore his sight, Ananias was skeptical. He knew how Saul was intent on destroying the church. But since Ananias was a faithful disciple of Jesus, he was obedient. Jesus had also revealed to Saul in a vision that Ananias was coming to lay hands on him so that he could restore his sight. God always gives us confirmation. He not only revealed to Ananias what to do, He revealed to Saul everything that Ananias was commanded to do.

In Acts 9:15–16 (NIV), the Lord said to Ananias, "Go! This man is My chosen instrument to carry My name before the Gentiles and their kings and before the people of Israel. I will show him how much he must suffer for My name."

Ananias was no longer skeptical. He obeyed the voice of the Lord. When he laid his hand on Saul, immediately something like scales fell from Saul's eyes and he could see again. Saul was filled with the Holy Spirit and he was baptized. He ate and regained his strength.

Jesus has given all of us as Christians a mission of lifting up Jesus. Remember, Saul was converted from persecuting Christians to promoting Jesus. We can promote Jesus by lifting Him up. Jesus says in John 12:32 (KJV), "And I, if I be lifted up from the earth, will draw all men unto Me."

The work of the cross is on the inside of us. Jesus wants us to promote Him by telling others about Him and by living in such a way that our light will shine before all men and women. Our lives will reveal the evidence of Jesus living inside us.

I read the story of a man who was a TV repairman.

Everybody in the neighborhood respected him because of his profession. One day a new family moved into the neighborhood. The man of the house, who was new to the neighborhood, had to install a new antenna on top of his house. He decided to model his antenna after his neighbor's, since his neighbor was a TV repairman. When the man climbed on top of his roof, he began fashioning his antenna exactly like his neighbor's. However, he noticed that the arm of the TV repairman's antenna was broken off. The new neighbor decided to break off the arm of his own antenna. He did not know that there had been a storm a month prior, and the storm had broken the arm off of the TV repairman's antenna, which he had not had time to fix. In modeling after the TV repairman's antenna, the new neighbor ended up with a defective antenna that worked poorly. His family was not pleased.

The moral of this story is that the world is watching us as Christians, and they are going to pattern their lives after us. Many times we walk around with broken lives that we have not turned over to Jesus so that He can make repairs. Our defective lives can hinder the walk of others around us, and God is going to hold us accountable.

POWER TO RISE AGAIN

Jesus died on the cross for our sins by shedding His blood; after three days, He rose again from the dead. The resurrection of Jesus is the premise of the Christian message. The same power that raised Jesus from the dead exists inside all of us as believers. Romans 8:11 (KJV) says, "But if the Spirit of Him that raised up Jesus from the dead dwell in you, He that raised up Christ from the dead shall also quicken your mortal bodies by His Spirit that dwelleth in you."

Resurrection power is not only for the hereafter, when we die and go to heaven; it is also for the here and now. God's resurrection power is on the inside of us, enabling us to be victorious in our daily lives. We are faced with trials and hardships repeatedly in this Christian journey, but the resurrection power of our Lord is working inside us. Some of the top problems that we deal with include the death of loved ones, marital problems or divorce, sickness or terminal illness, financial problems, and unexpected trauma. Whatever the dilemma, God has provided all the power that we need in order to overcome. The power of the Holy Spirit gives us joy. The Bible says in Nehemiah 8:10 (KJV) that the joy of the Lord is our strength.

We have the power to rise again from any of life's blows. Jesus says in John 11:25–26 (NIV): "I am the resurrection and the life. He who believes in Me will live, even though he dies; and whoever lives and believes in Me will never die. Do you believe this?"

Whenever Jesus says, "I Am," He is defining His character; He is identifying who He is, and He is declaring what He will do. As the resurrection and the life, Jesus assures us that we will never die in any season of life. When this earthly life is over and life leaves our physical body, we transition into the presence of God. The Apostle Paul says that to be absent from the body is to be present with the Lord—II Corinthians 5:8. The resurrection power of Jesus is on the inside of us, and we never really die. Eternity cannot be eradicated; it is forever. Jesus inside of us is eternity reigning in our mortal beings.

But what about the here and now, when we feel literally destroyed by overwhelming circumstances? This is the time when the resurrection power of Jesus will rise up inside us and give us a resurgence of life. We must not suppress the life force that exists within us that Jesus has come to earth to give us.

According to *Vine's Concise Dictionary of Bible Words*, the word "resurrection," which comes from the Greek word *anastasis*, means:

- A process of rising up
- Life after death
- To cause to stand

Just like the grave could not keep Jesus down, the problems of life will not keep us down, because of the resurrection power within us. Hold your head up high and continue to do what God has called you to do. God has placed greatness inside of you, but you must press on in order to achieve that greatness.

We must experience what Christ experienced in order to be crucified with Him. Galatians 2:20 (NIV) says, "I have been crucified with Christ and I no longer live, but Christ lives in me. The life I live in the body, I live by faith in the Son of God, who loved me and gave Himself for me."

Every year during the Easter season, each person in the congregation writes their name on a Post-it note and puts it on the cross. This is symbolic of nailing ourselves to the cross and being crucified with Jesus Christ. We surrender our lives to Jesus and re-dedicate our hearts to Him. We realize that it is no longer we who live, but Christ who lives on the inside of us. We live this life by faith and not by sight. We know that the devil will attack us profusely as we make our claim of being crucified with Christ. Nevertheless, Jesus has provided all that we need to stand up to the devil; we can resist him and he will flee from us (James 4:7 KJV). We must keep our focus on the cross, expecting the power of the Holy Spirit to guide us.

In acknowledging the resurrection power inside us, we have the same power that raised Jesus from the dead. We can personally apply the story of the resurrection of Jesus to our own lives. In Luke 24:1, we see that there was power to roll the stone away. God sent the angels to roll back the stone. The grave could not hold Jesus. This symbolizes the way in which the power of God operating inside us *opens closed doors* in our lives.

Luke 24:1–3 (NIV) says: "On the first day of the week, very early in the morning, the women took the spices they had prepared and went to the tomb. They found the stone rolled away from the tomb, but when they entered, they did not find the body of the Lord Jesus."

These women were the first to witness that Jesus had risen from the dead, making them the first missionaries. They had come to the tomb to anoint Jesus's body with spices, since the Jews did not practice embalming. This action demonstrated their love and devotion to Jesus. On their way to the tomb, they wondered who would help them roll away the stone. But to their surprise, the stone had already been rolled away by an angel (Matthew 28:2 KJV). This miracle is indicative of how Jesus opens doors for us in our time of need. Revelation 3:7 (KJV) says, "And to the angel of the church in Philadelphia write; These things saith He that is holy, He that is true, He that hath the key of David, He that openeth, and no man shutteth; and shutteth and no man openeth."

The use of the word "key" indicates that Jesus holds the key to every door and will unlock doors that lead to opportunities. He gives us the authority to open these doors by speaking to the situation. What Jesus opens, no one can shut, and what He shuts no one can open. We must believe that Jesus is the one who opens or closes doors for us.

When I was in college, my father, Thomas Bob Ross,

applied for a higher-paying position as a foreman at a company that made typewriter ribbon. He felt unqualified because he had not graduated from high school, and he had no experience as a foreman. Many of the other people applying for the job had completed high school, and some had earned some college credits. The one thing my dad had in His favor was the grace of God, and he had many years of experience in factory work. My dad was also a good reader. He could process information quickly and in an intelligent manner. Well, you probably guessed it: my dad passed the test with flying colors, and he got the foreman position. Despite the doubters, God is the one who opened the door of opportunity for my dad. God provided the mental sharpness for him to pass a test at that level. Remember, God will roll the stones away in our lives and provide unique opportunities for us. We only have to trust in Him with all our hearts and lean not on our own understanding, as stated in Proverbs 3:5–6 (KJV).

Resurrection power means that we have the power to leave the old behind. This is indicative of Jesus leaving His burial clothes behind at the tomb. Luke 24:5–8 (NIV) says: "In their fright the women bowed down with their faces to the ground, but the men said to them, 'Why do you look for the living among the dead? He is not here; He has risen! Remember how He told you, while He was still with you in Galilee: "The Son of Man must be delivered into the hands of sinful men, be crucified, and on the third day be raised again."' Then they remembered His words."

The women were afraid when they saw that Jesus was no longer in the tomb and that His grave clothes were left behind. The grave clothes that were left behind were symbolic that we must leave the old nature behind because we are new in Christ Jesus. II Corinthians 5:17 (NIV) says, "Therefore, if anyone is in Christ, he is a new creation; the old has gone, the new has come!" This means that we experience a total metamorphosis. We are literally a new creation.

Since we are new in Christ Jesus, we must not return to a life of sin. Romans 6:11, 14 (NIV) says, "Count yourselves dead to sin but alive to God in Christ Jesus. Therefore do not let sin reign in your mortal body so that you obey the evil desires. For sin shall not be your master."

When Jesus left His grave clothes behind, it symbolized the fact that He was no longer under the law. Although Jesus never sinned, He was born into sin by being born of a woman and born under the law. When He said on the cross, "It is finished," he meant that the old system of things was finished. We are now under grace. The old has gone and the new has come. We are free in Jesus Christ. We must not let sin master our bodies any more. We are now slaves of righteousness—our righteousness is in Jesus Christ because of grace!

Because of the resurrection power operating inside of us, we have the power to go forth as witnesses. I mentioned that the women were the first missionaries. Luke 24:9–10 (NIV) says: "When they came back from the tomb, they told all these things to the Eleven and to all the others. It was Mary Magdalene, Joanna, Mary the mother of James, and the others with them who told this to the apostles."

We can see from this passage that the women went forth to tell what they had witnessed. They told their experience to everyone they approached in their journey. Mary, the mother of Jesus, was not present in this group. It is believed that she was with John the Apostle, whom Jesus had instructed to take care of His mother. Jesus gave John this charge when He was dying on the cross (John 19:26–27, KJV).

When the ladies told the apostles what they had witnessed, the men did not believe them. Luke 24:11–12 (NIV) says: "But they did not believe the women, because their words seemed to them like nonsense. Peter, however, got up and ran to the tomb. Bending over, he saw the strips of linen lying by themselves, and he went away, wondering to himself what had happened."

Although the apostles had been with Jesus for three years, they did not remember what He had told them. He had said that He would be delivered into the hands of sinful men, be crucified, and on the third day be raised again. Since they did not remember Jesus's words—let alone the words of the prophets in the Old Testament—they were afraid and confused. Jesus had told them in Luke 24:25–27 (NLT), "You foolish people! You find it so hard to believe all that the prophets wrote in the Scriptures. Wasn't it clearly predicted that the Messiah would have to suffer all these things before entering His glory?" Luke goes on: "Then Jesus took them through the writing of Moses and all the prophets, explaining from all the Scriptures the things concerning Himself."

Jesus was with His apostles and His other followers for forty days before He ascended into heaven. He gave them this instruction, found in Acts 1:8 (NIV): "But you will receive power when the Holy Spirit comes on you; and you will be My witnesses in Jerusalem, and in all Judea and Samaria, and to the ends of the earth."

With this instruction, Jesus gave every believer the charge to go forth and be witnesses for Him. We are all missionaries, given the power and command to go forth and be witnesses!

If you don't know Jesus as your Lord and personal Savior, and you want to be a witness for Him, just pray the following sinner's prayer. After praying this prayer, connect with your spiritual leader, be baptized and live a life for Jesus!

THE SINNER'S PRAYER

Lord, Jesus, I am a sinner.

Please forgive me of all my sins and cleanse me from all unrighteousness.

I believe that You died for me on the cross and that You rose again.

Come now, Lord Jesus, and live Your life in me.

Fill me, Lord, with Your Holy Spirit.

Thank You, Lord, for saving me.

In Jesus' name I pray. Amen.

CHAPTER SIX

WINNING THROUGH GOD'S GRACE

And God is able to make all grace abound toward you, that you, always having all sufficiency in all things, may have an abundance for every good work.

II CORINTHIANS 9:8 (NKJV)

God's amazing grace enables us to win in every season or round of our lives. The word "grace" comes from the Greek word, *charis,* which means unearned favor and enablement from God. God's grace is utterly amazing; it is overwhelming and wonderful. When I think of the universal nature of grace, I am reminded of the apps on my iPhone. "App" is an abbreviation for "application"—software that performs specific functions on an electronic device. For special resources or programs that I need, usually I can say, "I have an app for that." This technological language means that all I have to do is press a tab or icon on my iPhone or laptop, and a world of information is made available to me. Grace is similar in scope. Whatever I need, grace is able to abound in every area of my life. Grace is at my disposal, benefiting me in whatever way is needed.

The initial phase of grace is salvation; we are saved by grace. Jesus died for us on the cross, ushering in a whole new dispensation called grace. We are no longer under the "Dispensation of the Law." We are under the "Dispensation of Grace." A dispensation is God's way of dealing with man during a particular period of time. Romans 5:8 (KJV) says, "But God commendeth His love toward us, in that, while we were yet sinners, Christ died for us."

Imagine such love. There was nothing required on our part; we had to do nothing for Jesus to die for us. We couldn't get ourselves right or make ourselves good enough for Jesus to come down from the comforts of heaven and die for us on the cross. Grace is the only answer for this act of love. Sin separates us from God. When Jesus died for us, His blood atoned for our sins. Leviticus 17:11b (KJV) says that it is the blood that makes atonement for one's life. Hebrews 9:22b (NLT) says: "For without the shedding of blood, there is no forgiveness." From these two verses of Scripture, we can see that it was necessary for Jesus to shed His blood on the cross so that our sins could be forgiven. The blood of Jesus reconciled us back to God the Father. Jesus is the only way to the Father. John 14:6 (KJV) says: "Jesus saith unto him, I am the way, the truth, and the life: No man cometh unto the Father, but by Me."

I read a story recently about two construction workers who fell into a pit. One construction worker said to the other, "Get me out of here. I hate it down here. It is cold and dark." The other worker responded, "You idiot! I am in the same plight as you. How in the world can I save you?"

Neither construction worker could help the other.

Suddenly a voice from above said: "Hello! Everything is going to be alright. Grab the rope and I will pull you up." A construction worker above the pit was able to rescue the other two. This heroic rescue was a picture of salvation. We could not save ourselves from the pit of hell. It is as if Jesus came down from heaven and said to us: "I will rescue you by dying on the cross. All you have to do is believe in Me and invite Me into your heart." Jesus came down from heaven to bring salvation to us. Romans 10:9–10 (NIV) says "that if you confess with your mouth, 'Jesus is Lord,' and believe in your heart that God raised Him from the dead, you will be saved. For it is with your heart that you believe and are justified, and it is with your mouth that you confess and are saved."

Whenever I am teaching the water baptism class for new membership at Hope Fellowship Church, I tell the candidates that they need to do two things. First, they need to verbally confess that Jesus is Lord, and second, they need to believe in their hearts that God raised Jesus from the dead. When I am teaching children, we physically touch our mouths and lay our hands on our hearts to repeat the Scripture in Romans 10:9–10. I tell them *that when we are saved, we use our mouths and our hearts—our mouths to say it and our hearts to believe it*. We say with our mouths that Jesus is Lord and we believe in our hearts that God raised Jesus from the dead. After that, we pray the Sinners Prayer that is included in each chapter in this book.

Ephesians 2:8–9 (NIV) says: "For it is by grace you have been saved, through faith—and this is not from yourselves, it is the gift of God—not by works, so that no one can boast." We cannot earn our salvation. It is one hundred percent free. Since we are set free from the law of sin and death, we need to stand in our salvation.

Galatians 5:1 (NKJV) says: "Stand fast therefore in the

liberty by which Christ has made us free, and do not be entangled again with a yoke of bondage."

The words "entangled again" come from the Greek word, *enecho,* which means to be held or caught. God does not want us to be held or caught by sin when we have been set free. We need to recognize that we are under a new covenant, the covenant of grace. We are saved by grace through faith. The law could not save us. Therefore, we need to walk in our freedom and not return to the confines of the law. The words "a yoke of bondage" mean observing any or all of the Mosaic laws, commandments, or rituals. If anyone goes back to keeping any aspect of the law, he or she is under obligation to keep the whole law.

Jesus did not come to destroy the law; He came to fulfill the law. Jesus said in Matthew 5:17 (NIV): "Do not think that I have come to abolish the Law or the Prophets; I have not come to abolish them but to fulfill them."

As Christians, let's stand in our freedom. Remember, freedom isn't free. Jesus died to pay for our freedom with His blood. He does not want anyone to go to hell, but He wants everyone to be saved.

A story is told about an old Native American Chief who had lived in sin for many years but had come to salvation during his older years. All of his friends and the people in his tribe noticed the change in him. One day when everyone was gathered around him, they asked him to explain the great change in his life. They asked him to explain what it meant to be saved.

The old chief stooped down on the ground and gathered many leaves and put them in a circular arrangement. After that, he put a worm in the center of the leaves. Then he got a match and lit the outer perimeter of the leaves and watched them burn. Right before the flames engulfed the worm, he snatched the worm from the burning flames.

Holding the worm gently in his hand, the chief exclaimed to the people, "Me, that worm! Me, that worm!"

You see, we are all sinners saved by grace (Romans 3:23–24 KJV). At just the right time, Jesus died for our sins—rescuing us from hell's flames. If you want to invite Jesus into your heart to be your Lord and personal savior, do that now. Just pray The Sinner's Prayer.

THE SINNER'S PRAYER

Lord, Jesus, I am a sinner.

Please forgive me of all my sins and cleanse me from all unrighteousness.

I believe that You died for me on the cross and that You rose again.

Come now, Lord Jesus, and live Your life in me.

Fill me, Lord, with Your Holy Spirit.

Thank You, Lord, for saving me.

In Jesus' name I pray. Amen.

Please contact a spiritual leader and continue your salvation walk by being baptized and living a life for Jesus.

GRACE FOR THE FIGHT

Now that you have invited Jesus into your heart, the devil will be hot on your trail, attempting to get you off the path of life. Don't worry. The grace of Jesus Christ has provided all the spiritual armor you need to fight this battle. As a matter of fact, the fight is fixed. We win! We are in this race to win it. Jesus won the battle over Satan when he died on Calvary and rose from the dead. We need to be watchful and fight the good fight.

I Peter 5:8 (NLT) says, "Stay alert! Watch out for your great enemy, the devil. He prowls around like a roaring lion, looking for someone to devour." The word "prowl" means to move around steadily, looking for prey. We must not become the devil's prey. He desires to viciously tear us apart. I Peter 5:9 (NLT) says, "Stand firm against him, and be strong in your faith. Remember that your Christian brothers and sisters all over the world are going through the same kind of suffering you are."

We are not alone. Other Christians are suffering just like we are. We must learn to stand in our spiritual armor. A good friend told me that we can measure the weight of our blow to Satan by the one we get back. This means that when we throw the devil a strong blow by advancing in God's Kingdom, he will throw a strong punch back at us. The devil is after our faith and our salvation. He does not want us to go to heaven. Ephesians 6:12 (NLT) says, "We are not fighting against flesh-and-blood enemies, but against evil rulers and authorities of the unseen world, against mighty powers in this dark world, and against evil spirits in the heavenly places."

Let's not deceive ourselves. We cannot use human artillery to defeat Satan. The battle we are fighting is a spiritual one. The Bible says in II Corinthians 10:3–5 (NIV): "For though we live in the world, we do not wage war as the world does. The weapons we fight with are not the weapons of the world. On the contrary, they have divine power to demolish strongholds. We demolish arguments and every pretension that sets itself up against the knowledge of God, and we take captive every thought to make it obedient to Christ."

The weapons we fight with are powerful and effective

because they are God's weaponry. As Christians, we can take negative thoughts captive and bring them into the obedience of Jesus Christ. For example, when the devil puts a negative thought in my mind, I say: "I hold that thought captive in the name of Jesus." The same applies to dreams; if I awaken in the night after having a bad dream, I say: "I hold that negative dream captive in the name of Jesus." I use my words to fight for me. Our words in the name of Jesus have power.

Because of grace, Jesus has provided all of the spiritual armor we need to stand against the devil. We must walk in our weapons of warfare. Ephesians 6:11 (KJV) says, "Put on the whole armour of God, that ye may be able to stand against the wiles of the devil."

The devil has schemes or strategies that are designed to make us fail. The devil plots continuously to cause our demise. Nevertheless, we must stand in faith and claim the victory that Jesus has already won. As we stand, we must be fully equipped in the armor that is described in Ephesians 6:10–17. We must take on the *Helmet of Salvation*—which protects our mind. As we stand in the assurance of our salvation, our minds are protected. The battleground is the mind. In the name of Jesus, no weapon formed against us shall prosper (Isaiah 54:17). We take on the *Breastplate of Righteousness*—our righteousness is from Jesus Christ. Our righteousness protects our heart and guides the actions. The heart is the seat of our moral activity, and we need to hide God's word in our heart so that we will not sin against Him (Psalm 119:11). We take on the *Belt of Truth*—our truth is in Jesus Christ. The truth holds us up and keeps us from falling. When we genuinely know the truth, the truth will set us free (John 8:32). We put on the *Shoes of the Gospel of Readiness*—our readiness to spread the Gospel provides shoes for our feet. These shoes are protected by the Gospel of peace. The shoes help us to walk in our freedom. We must take up the *Sword of the Spirit*—which is the word of God. The Sword of the Spirit is our offensive weapon, meaning that we can go after the devil by saying, "It is written." The other pieces of armor are for defensive battle—meaning that we can stand our ground and prevent Satan from advancing into God's Kingdom. We take on the *Shield of Faith*—our faith is our shield, which wards off the devil's flaming arrows. The Roman soldiers' shields were covered with leather, and could be soaked in water to put out the flaming arrows of the enemy. Our faith is soaked in the water of the Holy Spirit, and can extinguish the flaming arrows of the enemy. I put on the armor in this order every day. By putting on every piece of armor, we can walk forth in the victory that God has intended for His children!

In Ephesians 6:13 (NIV), we are told to: "Put on the full armor of God, so that when the day of evil comes, you may be able to stand your ground, and after you have done everything, to stand."

The day of evil will come. When that day comes, we are already suited with the armor that God has provided for us through the finished work of Jesus Christ on the cross. An important form of armor to walk in is *Prayer.* Ephesians 6:18 (NIV) says, "And pray in the Spirit on all occasions with all kinds of prayers and requests. With this in mind, be alert and always keep on praying for all the saints."

We need each other as we pray for one another. So many times we hear the expression: "I've got your back." One way we can have each other's backs is to pray for each other. The Bible says to pray with all kinds of prayers; some types of prayers are adoration, confession, thanksgiving, and supplication. Let's never stop praying (I Thessalonians 5:17).

GRACE WHEN GOD SAYS "NO"!

Has God told you "no" recently? How did it feel? The negative answers from God can either make us or break us. We can definitely determine whether we are spiritual by this type of response from God. We must remember that God is the Father and we are the children; He is the Creator and we are the created. He knows what is best for us. The answer "no" from God might be God's final answer regarding a particular situation, but it is not His final work. We must allow God to be God. Perhaps we were praying for God to heal someone and that person died. Does that shake your faith? Are you tempted to rebel or show respect? These situations are a barometer of where we are spiritually.

In order to allow difficult situations to shape us, we must trust in the Lord. The word "trust" means to rely on. Proverbs 3:5–6 (NIV) says: "Trust in the Lord with all your heart and lean not on your own understanding. In all your ways acknowledge Him, and He will make your paths straight."

When we choose to trust in the Lord, we are demonstrating that we are surrendering to His Lordship. Our understanding is so limited that we should not look to our wisdom as a support system. Our wisdom and understanding must be from God. Once we truly recognize that God is the master of our ship, we will commit our ways to Him. I am reminded of a box of crayons. When children are small, there are two things they must learn about crayons—they must learn to choose the right color, and they must learn to color within the lines. In the same way, we must learn to trust in the Lord. We must learn to choose the right steps to take in life, by following the will and plan of God for our lives. We must learn to stay within the lines of His will, by obeying His voice. We must stay within the boundaries that God has established for us.

God is Sovereign, and we must learn to look to Him as our Supreme ruler. Isaiah 40:10 (KJV) says: "Behold, the Lord God will come with strong hand, and His arm shall rule for Him: Behold, His reward is with Him, and His work before Him."

God's arm is almighty and we must allow His Sovereign power to work for us. I have known people who say, "Well, I will trust in my rabbit's foot as my good luck charm." I can assure you that a rabbit's foot will not bring you good luck. Remember, it was not good luck for the rabbit!

God's thoughts are so much higher than ours. Isaiah 55:8–9 (NIV) says, "For My thoughts are not your thoughts, neither are your ways My ways," declares the Lord. "As the heavens are higher than the earth, so are My ways higher than your ways and My thoughts than your thoughts."

Let's consider the distance the heavenly bodies are from the earth. For instance, the sun is 93 million miles from the earth, and it is the closest star. Yes, the sun is a star. If the sun is the closest star, imagine how far the other stars are from us. Well, as far as the heavens are from the earth, so are God's ways and thoughts higher than ours. We can't even wrap our intellect around the wisdom of God. That dynamic alone is enough for me to totally trust God. Many times I tell God, "I don't know what you are doing, but I know that it will be good!" Then, I leave it there.

The Bible says in II Peter 3:8 (NLT): "But you must not forget this one thing, dear friends: A day is like a thousand years to the Lord, and a thousand years is like a day."

Life may appear to be long for us. But if a person is one hundred years old, it is still early morning of one day with God. God has planned every moment in time that He has designed for us. Our suffering is designed to make us stronger and to equip us for the next chapter in our lives. God knows what He is doing. Our pain is for our gain.

I heard this story about a little boy who was three years

old and very sick. He was in the hospital and had undergone numerous tests and procedures due to his illness. The doctors had scheduled a spinal tap, and the mother talked to her young son in advance to prepare him. She told him, "Son, this will be painful; but remember the doctors love you and I love you. The hurting will make you better."

The day for the spinal tap arrived and the young boy was brave. The pain was horrendous; it took three nurses to hold his body still. After everything was over, he looked up at the doctor and said, "Doctor, thank you for my hurting."

The young boy knew in his heart that the hurting made him better. Wouldn't it be remarkable if we trusted God enough to thank Him for our hurting? Romans 8:28 says that we know that in all things God works for the good of those who love Him, who have been called according to His purpose. This Scripture communicates to us that God is working everything out according to His master plan. He knows how every piece of experience is part of the whole picture.

The Apostle Paul was troubled when God told him "no" concerning his thorn in the flesh. Paul's thorn in the flesh was a severe affliction that he was suffering. The Scriptures do not reveal what this specific affliction was, but we know that Paul asked God to remove it from him, and God said that His grace was sufficient for him. This story is told in II Corinthians 12:1–10 (NIV). Three things occurred in Paul's life in order for him to process this divine response.

ASSESSMENT

The Apostle Paul had to use the proper assessment concerning what God was doing in his life. To assess something is to evaluate it. So Paul started with the visions God had disclosed to him in his dreams. The Bible says in II Corinthians 12:1–2 (NIV): "I must go on boasting. Although there is nothing to be gained, I will go on to visions and revelations from the Lord. I know a man in Christ who fourteen years ago was caught up to the third heaven. Whether it was in the body or out of the body I do not know—God knows."

When Paul said that he knew a man "caught up to the third heaven," he was talking about himself. God literally revealed things of glory to him, things that were difficult to fathom. Paul waited fourteen years before mentioning this mysterious experience. He pondered these visions and revelations in his heart until disclosing this information in the letter to the Corinthians.

Paul continued this dialog in II Corinthians 12:3–4 (NIV) by saying: "And I know that this man—whether in the body or apart from the body I do not know, but God knows—was caught up to paradise. He heard inexpressible things, things that man is not permitted to tell."

Paul was uniquely touched by God. He was caught up to paradise or heaven. He saw things that cannot be uttered in words. Paul felt that he would be boasting to tell about such things; but nevertheless, he would boast if God would get the glory.

In II Corinthians 12:5 (NIV), Paul says: "I will boast about a man like that, but I will not boast about myself, except my weaknesses."

When Paul boasted about his weaknesses, he was glorifying God. He was trying to affirm his apostleship in the midst of false teachers. Many false teachers had questioned his authority as an apostle, and he was trying to affirm his credibility. As Paul assessed his thorn in the flesh and his dreams and visions, he concluded that he would only boast about what God was doing through him.

ALIGNMENT

In order to process God's negative response, the apostle Paul had to come into alignment with God's will. The word "alignment" means to line up with or to arrange into a line; it means to stay within the boundaries. Paul had to continue to stand on the sovereignty of God. Paul refrained from boasting about the dreams and visions because he didn't want people to think too highly of him. He had to stay in his lane and give God the glory. He knew that the thorn in the flesh was given to him so that he would not become conceited and boastful.

The Bible says in II Corinthians 12:6–8 (NIV): "Even if I should choose to boast, I would not be a fool, because I would be speaking the truth. But I refrain, so no one will think more of me than is warranted by what I do or say. To keep me from becoming conceited because of these surpassing great revelations, there was given me a thorn in my flesh, a messenger to Satan, to torment me. Three times I pleaded with the Lord to take it away from me."

The King James Bible uses the word "buffet" instead of "torment." The word "buffet" means to strike against repeatedly. God gave Satan permission to torment Paul. The enemy can do nothing to us without God's permission. No one knows exactly what the thorn in the flesh was, but scholars have concluded that it was a chronic, debilitating physical affliction. This thorn in the flesh kept Paul humble, and he was constantly asking God for help and guidance. This affliction did not prevent Paul from spreading the Gospel to countless people. Paul said that he pleaded with the Lord three times to take the thorn away, but God denied his request.

In order to process God's negative response, Paul had to give God the proper acclaim. The word "acclaim" means praise and strong approval. Paul had to remember to give God praise through it all. He came to understand that God's grace was sufficient for us in our weaknesses.

Paul says in II Corinthians 12:9–10 (NIV): "But He said to me, 'My grace is sufficient for you, for My power is made perfect in weakness.' Therefore I will boast all the more gladly about my weaknesses, so that Christ's power may rest on me. That is why, for Christ's sake, I delight in weaknesses, in insults, in hardships, in persecutions, in difficulties. For when I am weak, then I am strong."

We must remember that God's grace is His enablement in us. His power is made perfect in our weakness. At our weakest point, we are our strongest in Christ's strength. Let's rely on the power of God to work in us. When we do that, we are witnessing grace in action in our lives. Grace is not only God's unearned favor toward us, it is His enablement in us. God by His grace enables us to do all that He has called us to do.

Whenever God says "no," He has a divine plan. The pain from the experience will polish us in our Christian growth. A lady was walking down the beach. She picked up a rock as she strolled along the shore. She noticed that the part of the rock that was hidden and pressed against the cove was sharp and pointed. But the part of the rock that was struck by the waves was smooth and polished.

This rock describes our lives. We are polished by the winds and waves of life. God uses painful experiences to shape us and make us conform to His glory.

CHAPTER SEVEN

WINNING THROUGH DEVOTION TO GOD

Guard my life, for I am devoted to You.

PSALM 86:2 (NIV)

To what are you devoted or to whom are you devoted? Your devotion will be evident by those things to which you gravitate, or by the people with whom you spend the most time. Whatever you are devoted to, that is where your loyalties will rest.

Here's a definition of the word "devoted," which comes from the Hebrew word *herem:*

- Separated and excluded; shut in
- Most holy; set apart to the Lord
- Belonging solely to God

Whatever is devoted to God belongs to God. Have you devoted yourself to God? True devotion means having God as the primary person to whom we are devoted. God must be first place in our lives. This does not mean that we are not devoted to others in our lives; it means that God is the center of all relationships. Our devotion to God will enable us to have successful relationships with family, friends and those in our sphere of influence. Devotion to others begins with our devotion to God. We cannot have divided devotion. We can only be devoted to one master. To be devoted to someone is a positional stance. We cannot be in two places at one time. The Bible says in Romans 12:1 (NIV): "Therefore, I urge you, brothers, in view of God's mercy, to offer your bodies as living sacrifices, holy and pleasing to God—this is your spiritual act of worship."

The word "offer" means to present for acceptance. When we offer ourselves to God, we are presenting ourselves to Him for His approval. He will not approve of us if our hearts are not truly yielded to Him. We please God with our faith. When we stand before Him in faith, and we surrender, he accepts our sacrifice. To truly devote ourselves to God is a sacrifice—we give ourselves away to God.

Paul, in his letter to Titus, told him to teach the people about living devoted lives, and devoting themselves to doing good. Titus 3:14 (KJV) says: "And let ours also learn to maintain good works for necessary uses, that they be not unfruitful."

In other words, people need to live productive lives, and the only way they can do this is by being devoted to doing good by serving the Lord. We cannot serve God and the world. We must make a choice. We demonstrate who we serve by how we live.

Jesus says in Matthew 6:24 (KJV), "No one can serve two masters: for either he will hate the one, and love the other; or else he will hold to the one, and despise the other. Ye cannot serve God and mammon."

The word "mammon" is used to denote riches and material wealth. It is a fact; we cannot serve both Jesus Christ and the riches of this world. When we try to serve both, we become frustrated. We can only demonstrate faithfulness to one master.

Joshua says we should choose whom we are going to serve. Joshua 24:15 (NIV) says, "But if serving the Lord seems undesirable to you, then choose for yourselves this day whom you will serve, whether the gods your forefathers served beyond the River, or the gods of the Amorites, in whose land you are living. But as for me and my household, we will serve the Lord."

What choice have you made? Will you and your household serve the Lord? Decide today. You cannot serve two masters. Living victoriously means serving God with our whole hearts, and having no other gods before Him.

There was a father who was always talking to his son about making choices. His son had a hard time choosing the right thing to do. One day the father put two chairs before his son and said, "Son, try to sit in both chairs." The boy could not do it. He fell between the two chairs. The father said that the same is true with life, you must make a decision or you will fall on your face. You cannot serve both Jesus and the world. Choose today whom you will serve.

THE DEVOTION OF A GODLY MOTHER

Devotion can be seen in the life of a Godly mother. On Mother's Day, I preached a sermon entitled, The Devotion of a Godly Mother. A Godly mother is innately devoted to her children and family, because of the power of the Holy Spirit dwelling within her. As a born-again woman, the devoted mother naturally separates herself unto those entrusted in her care with the help and guidance from the Holy Spirit. She trains her children as instructed by the Lord. Since the Godly mother loves the Lord, she can sacrificially love her family. Abraham Lincoln once said, "No man is poor who has a Godly mother."

The above statement is profoundly true. As the second oldest child of a family of fourteen children, I can attest that a Godly mother enriches a home. The qualities that my mother instilled into my siblings and myself are priceless. When I was younger, all I could see were the struggles and hardships. I did not envision the long-term effect of how the love of my Godly mother could overshadow all of those obstacles. Anytime I mention my mother, I have to simultaneously mention my father, because they shared the parenting role. Over time, I came to recognize that my mother (Mary Anna Ross) and my father (Thomas Bob Ross) instilled character traits that would eternally impact the world around us. Material possessions were not in abundance, but love made us the richest children in southeastern Missouri.

I can attribute my strong prayer life and life of faith to the practice of my parents. They did not just tell us to pray and have faith; they demonstrated it. The Godly example they modeled made all the difference in the lives of their children. The Bible says in Proverbs 22:6 (KJV): "Train up a child in the way he should go: and when he is old, he will not depart from it."

The words "train up" come from the Hebrew word, *hanak,* which basically means the following: to dedicate or devote to God, and to give discipline and instruction.

In the Hebrew rendition of the words "train up," we are to give our children back to God. Whatever is devoted or dedicated to the Lord belongs to the Lord. It is impossible to give our children to the Lord if we are not devoted to the Lord ourselves. Whatever we give to God is holy and set apart.

God expects us as parents to discipline our children and give them instruction. They are God's property. Proverbs 29:15 (KJV) says: "The rod and reproof give wisdom: but a child left to himself bringeth his mother to shame."

All parents should have methods of discipline; children should not be left on their own to provide their own set of rules. If we leave our children to themselves, they will disgrace us. The word "disgrace" means to dishonor or lose respect. We have our responsibilities as parents, and children have their responsibilities as children. Ephesians 6:1–3 (NIV) says: "Children, obey your parents in the Lord, for this is right. Honor your father and mother—which is the first commandment with a promise—that it may go well with you and that you may enjoy long life on the earth."

Children need to obey and honor their parents; then they will be blessed and have long life on the earth. I heard my mother say to one of my siblings, "I am just as much your mother at your age of fifty as I was when you were a newborn baby." What a true statement. Our parents are always our parents and we are always their children—regardless of age.

Godly mothers must remain Godly so that their children will have spiritual examples. Children watch what their mothers do and pattern their lives after them. Proverbs 31:28–29 (NIV) says: "Her children arise and call her blessed; her husband also, and he praises her: 'Many women do noble things, but you surpass them all.'"

When mothers live virtuously, their children and husbands will compliment them. I was told a comical story about a mother who had raised three sons as a single mom. Life was difficult for her, but her devoted parenting paid off. Her boys all succeeded in life and became affluent. For

Mother's Day, one of this mother's sons gave her a new car; another one bought her some expensive gifts for her house. The third really wanted to impress his mother; so he bought her an expensive parrot. This parrot could recite the entire Bible. It could name the chapter and verse of Scriptures. It was remarkable!

The mother sat down one day to write thank you letters to her sons. To each one she communicated her heartfelt appreciation. To the son who gave her the parrot she said: "Son, thank you so very much. What a delightful gift. I enjoyed your gift so much. That chicken sure was delicious!"

What a comical story! Nevertheless, she enjoyed her gift. This mother expressed gratitude to each son equally.

QUALITIES OF A GODLY WOMAN

1. She perseveres.

The word "persevere" means to persist in spite of obstacles. Hannah exemplified this virtue when she tolerated the torturing remarks from her rival, Peninnah. Samuel 1:4–6 (NIV) says: "Whenever the day came for Elkanah to sacrifice, he would give portions of the meat to his wife Peninnah and to all her sons and daughters. But to Hannah he gave a double portion because he loved her, and the Lord had closed her womb. And because the Lord had closed her womb, her rival kept provoking her in order to irritate her."

It was required by the Jewish law that Jewish males would travel to Shiloh—the religious center of the nation—to celebrate the three feast days, three times a year. Elkanah and his family traveled from Ramah to Shiloh to worship and offer sacrifices to God at the tabernacle. Elkanah was married to Hannah and Peninnah. It was during these feast days that the taunting from Peninnah intensified.

Having two wives posed numerous problems and rivalry. Although polygamy was not God's design, the custom of that day permitted it in order for families to produce more offspring for the work force. Having many children was a symbol of status and wealth. A woman who was barren in this culture was considered to be a failure. Hannah was reminded of her shortcomings by the constant badgering of Peninnah, who had at least ten sons. Elkanah reassured Hannah of his love for her by telling her that he was more kind to her than ten sons would have been (I Samuel 1:8). Elkanah gave Hannah a double portion of the meat that was offered during the sacrifice. The name "Hannah" means "Woman of Grace." I am sure that Peninnah was threatened by the graciousness of Elkanah toward Hannah. Therefore, she provoked Hannah even more, causing Hannah to weep bitterly. I Samuel 1:7 (NIV) says: "This went on year after year. Whenever Hannah went up to the house of the Lord, her rival provoked her till she wept and would not eat."

2. She prays.

Hannah literally became ill due to Peninnah's hurtful and demeaning remarks. The tremendous pain drove Hannah to her knees. We must remember that whenever troubles seem to overwhelm us, we can always go to God in prayer.

Prayer is drawing near to God and making our petitions known to Him. I Samuel 1:9–11 (NIV) says: "Once when they had finished eating and drinking in Shiloh, Hannah stood up. Now Eli the priest was sitting on a chair by the doorpost of the Lord's temple. In bitterness of soul Hannah wept much and prayed to the Lord. And she made a vow, saying, 'O Lord Almighty, if You will only look upon Your servant's misery and remember me, and not forget Your servant but give her a son, then I will give him to the Lord for all the days of his life, and no razor will ever be used on his head.'"

Hannah made a Nazarite vow, promising to God that she would give her son back to Him and no razor would ever be used on his head. This was a life-long commitment. She made a vow to set her son aside for God's service for life. Hannah refers to God as "Lord Almighty," which means Lord of Hosts. This means that God is the God of all armies, and there are no other powers above the strength of God. Hannah had to begin with the foundational truth that God is sovereign. In her weeping before God, she gained hope and strength. God touched Hannah in a mighty way.

As Eli observed Hannah's motions of prayer, he thought she was drunk. Her mouth was moving, but no words came forth. Hannah reassured him that she was not drunk, only deeply distressed. The words were on her heart, but she could not utter them. Someone once told me that in prayer, it is better to have a heart without words than words without a heart. Hannah's words were from the heart, and God heard her. When she arose from her knees, she knew that she had received victory. She was able to eat and be strengthened. Eli reassured her in I Samuel 1:17 (NIV) by saying: "Go in peace, and may the God of Israel grant you what you have asked of Him."

God did grant to Hannah what she had asked of Him. Shortly after that time, she conceived. God delights in answering the prayers of His children. We must not give up, despite the barriers that are before us. God honors our faith. Hebrews 11:6 (KJV) says: "But without faith it is impossible to please Him: for he that cometh to God must believe that He is, and that He is a rewarder of them that diligently seek Him."

God rewarded Hannah's faith in a tremendous way. He gave her a son, Samuel, who helped to restore Israel to a state of wholeness and Godliness.

Samuel was Israel's last judge, and he was a priest and prophet.

3. She produces.

To "produce" means to give birth to or to bring forth. Hannah produced when her focus was redirected back on God. She maintained her state of hope and faith and she conceived. I Samuel 1:20 (NIV) says: "So in the course of time Hannah conceived and gave birth to a son. She named him Samuel, saying, "Because I asked the Lord for him."

God answered Hannah's prayer. I love the meaning of Samuel's name—"Because I asked the Lord for him." Samuel's name is a name of faith. In my personal life, when I get up off my knees, I have the attitude that I have asked the Lord and I know that He is going to answer. Everyone goes through times of barrenness, those times when nothing seems to work. There are times when all doors appear to be closed, and jobs and opportunities are not present. There are times when money is so scarce that discouragement burrows itself into our hearts. During those times of dryness and emptiness, we must remember that delays are not denials. Faith and hope must prevail. Faith is believing without seeing; it is having the confidence that God is going to do what He says. Hope is the expectation that something good is going to happen. Faith and hope must co-exist.

After Samuel was born, Hannah did not go up to Shiloh with her husband Elkanah. I Samuel 1:21–22; 27–28 (NIV) says: "When the man Elkanah went up with all his family to offer the annual sacrifice to the Lord and to fulfill his vow, Hannah did not go. She said to her husband, 'After the boy is weaned, I will take him and present him before the Lord, and he will live there always. I prayed for this child, and the Lord has granted me what I asked of Him. So now I give him to the Lord. For his whole life he will be given over to the Lord.' And he worshiped the Lord there."

Samuel was weaned at the age of three years old. At that time, Hannah took him to the temple and gave him back to the Lord for service, as she had vowed. Hannah visited Samuel frequently, and every year she made him a robe like the one that Eli possessed.

4. She praises.

Praise is what we do in response to God's goodness and faithfulness. Hannah offered thanksgiving to God for answering her prayer by giving her a son, Samuel. Hannah says in I Samuel 2:1-2 (KJV): "And Hannah prayed, and said, My heart rejoiceth in the Lord, mine horn is exalted in the Lord: my mouth is enlarged over mine enemies; because I rejoice in Thy salvation. There is none holy as the Lord: for there is none beside Thee: neither is there any rock like our God."

Hannah used her heart and mouth to express her thanks and praise to God. She rejoiced in her heart and she boasted of the Lord with her mouth. She said that her horn was lifted up, which meant that God had delivered her from a position of disgrace to a state of honor and strength. Hannah is thrilled about God's deliverance.

Hannah said that God was her rock. The word "rock" is a metaphor to depict the strength and stability of God. God is our unfailing source of security and power. He is the foundation upon which we should always stand. When we praise God, we give Him our voice of approval and adoration. God delights in the praises of His people.

God blessed Hannah to give birth to other children. In I Samuel 2:21 (KJV), it says: "And the Lord visited Hannah, so that she conceived, and bore three sons and two daughters. And the child Samuel grew before the Lord."

The Lord blessed Hannah with six children, including Samuel. This is an encouraging story for those of us who may be barren in any manner—whether we are trying to conceive a child or attempting to give birth to a ministry. God gives the increase. Everything that is produced must begin with God. Whatever God produces, He blesses. All births must have the proper gestation period, the period of time for carrying the unborn. Whether we are referring to an unborn child or an unborn dream, God will enable us to give birth at the proper time.

POWER TO LIVE THE DEVOTED LIFE

Are you a born-again Christian? If so, the power to live the devoted life exists inside of you. We don't ask God for what we already have. We have the power; what we need to do is unleash it. I am reminded of two balloons, one with helium inside and floating in the air, and the other with no helium. The helium-filled balloon will ascend to great heights, representing life in the Spirit. But the plain balloon with no air inside remains lifeless, representing life without the Spirit. These two balloons are indicative of our lives with or without the Spirit. The Holy Spirit enables us to ascend and be all that God has created us to be. It is in God that we live and move and have our being (Acts 17:28). Without God and His Holy Spirit, we can do nothing. Like the balloon without the helium, we cannot accomplish our purpose without the wind of the Holy Spirit.

The Apostle Paul prayed constantly for the people that he ministered to from day to day. In Ephesians 3:20 (NKJV), Paul offers a prayer that is often used as a benediction. It says: "Now to Him who is able to do exceedingly abundantly above all that we ask or think, according to the power that works in us."

The word "exceedingly" means to go beyond limits; "abundantly" means to have great quantity; and "above" means a higher place. In assimilating these words together for our lives, God is able to take us beyond limits to a higher place with great blessings. Our minds cannot conceive the magnitude of blessings that God has in store for us because of His power that works inside of us. My prayer is that we as Christians will grasp the concept of the depths of this power.

Paul continues to pray for the people in Ephesians 1:19–20 (NLT). He says: "I also pray that you will understand the incredible greatness of God's power for us who believe Him. This is the same mighty power that raised Christ from the dead and seated Him in the place of honor at God's right hand in the heavenly realms."

The word "understand" means to comprehend the meaning of and to have thorough knowledge of. This type of understanding comes from the Greek word, *ginosko,* which means to understand completely and to come into relationship. Paul's prayer is that God's people will understand the incredible power that is available for us as Christians. The same power that raised Jesus from the dead is available inside of us. We can say with confidence, "I can do all things through Christ, who strengthens me" Philippians 4:13 (NKJV).

The power to live the devoted life was promised by

Jesus. Jesus says in John 14:16–17 (NIV), "And I will ask the Father, and He will give you another Counselor to be with you forever—the Spirit of truth. The world cannot accept Him, because it neither sees Him nor knows Him. But you know Him, for He lives with you and will be in you."

The Holy Spirit is called our "Paraclete," which means one who comes alongside. In the past, during times of war, soldiers went to battle in pairs. One person was called the paraclete. During battle, the paraclete would stand side by side or back to back when needed, protecting his partner from behind. No danger would come upon him, because the paraclete protected him. The Holy Spirit stands side by side and back to back with us, protecting us and guiding us. He guides us into all truth.

Another instance in the Bible where Jesus promised us the Holy Spirit is found in Acts 1:4–5, 8 (NIV), which reads: "Do not leave Jerusalem, but wait for the gift My Father promised, which you have heard Me speak about. For John baptized with water, but in a few days you will be baptized with the Holy Spirit . . . But you will receive power when the Holy Spirit comes on you; and you will be My witnesses in Jerusalem, and in all Judea and Samaria, and to the ends of the earth."

In this scene, Jesus is talking to His apostles before ascending into heaven, before the Day of Pentecost. He is trying to prepare them for the power that was preparing to come upon them. The apostles, some women (including Jesus's mother), and other followers were in the upper room of a large house, praying for ten days—and then the power came upon them.

The power to live the devoted life prevailed at Pentecost. The word "prevailed" means that the Holy Spirit was poured out upon the people, and it was widespread. Acts 2:1–4 (NIV) says: "When the day of Pentecost came, they were all together in one place. Suddenly a sound like the blowing of a violent wind came from heaven and filled the whole house where they were sitting. They saw what seemed to be tongues of fire that separated and came to rest on each of them. All of them were filled with the Holy Spirit and began to speak in other tongues as the Spirit enabled them."

The men and women in the upper room were filled with the Holy Spirit and began to speak in an unknown tongue. Tongues of fire were upon their heads. The fire is symbolic of God's purifying presence. Fire burns undesirable elements that are in our lives. The fire of the Holy Spirit sets our hearts aflame to ignite the lives of others. God is a consuming fire (Hebrews 12:29, KJV).

Thousands of people were in Jerusalem because of the feast of Pentecost, also called the feast of First Harvest. This feast is one of the three feasts that Jewish males were required to celebrate. The crowd was already present for the huge harvest of souls that resulted from Pentecost.

Here's a definition of the word "Pentecost," which comes from the Greek word *pentekostos*:

- Fifty or fiftieth day
- Fifty days after Easter
- Birthday of the church
- The coming of the Holy Spirit

The believers in the upper room began to speak in other tongues as the Holy Spirit enabled them. The key word is "enabled." We cannot speak in an unknown tongue unless the Holy Spirit gives us the ability. Zechariah 4:6 (KJV) says: "Not by might, nor by power, but by my Spirit, saith the Lord of hosts."

The power to live the devoted life was practiced by

believers. After Peter was filled with the Holy Spirit, he preached to the international crowd, and more than three thousand people were saved. Acts 2:14–18 (NLT) says: "Then Peter stepped forward with the eleven other apostles and shouted to the crowd, 'Listen carefully, all of you, fellow Jews and residents of Jerusalem! Make no mistake about this. These people are not drunk, as some of you are assuming. Nine o'clock in the morning is much too early for that. No, what you see was predicted long ago by the prophet Joel: 'In the last days,' God says, 'I will pour out My Spirit upon all people. Your sons and daughters will prophesy. Your young men will see visions, and your old men will dream dreams. In those days I will pour out My Spirit even on My servants—men and women alike—and they will prophesy.'"

Peter delivered a powerful message on the Day of Pentecost. As we think about Peter's actions, we can attest that only the Holy Spirit can give such boldness. Peter was transformed. Only the Holy Spirit can render such results. Acts 2:41 (NIV) says: "Those who accepted his (Peter's) message were baptized, and about three thousand were added to their number that day."

As people witnessed the actions of Peter and the other apostles, the Bible says in Acts 2:43 that everyone was filled with awe, and many wonders and miraculous signs were done by the apostles. This power is available for us today. Jesus gives us the promise in Mark 16:17–18 (NKJV): "And these signs will follow those who believe: In My name they will cast out demons; they will speak with new tongues; they will take up serpents; and if they drink anything deadly, it will by no means hurt them; they will lay hands on the sick, and they will recover."

Those of us who have invited Jesus into our hearts to be our Lord and personal Savior qualify for these signs.

Jesus says that these signs will follow those who believe. We must believe in the finished work of Jesus Christ and believe that He is able to do everything that He has promised. The authority is in the name of Jesus. Let's trust in His name, not in our own names and shortcomings.

I read a story once about a lady who was sharing her Christian experience with a friend. She said, "There are times when I feel like a bucket with holes in it. I get filled with the Holy Spirit and I feel really good. Then after a few days or weeks, I feel drained."

The lady's friend remarked, "Yes, but even a bucket with holes in it will stay full if you immerse it in the river and leave it there."

This describes what we must do if we are going to remain walking in the fullness of the Spirit. With all of our day-to-day cares and drama, we can become drained and depleted of strength. This is why Jesus tells us to abide in Him and He will abide in us; then we will bear much fruit (John 15:5). The abiding in Jesus keeps us in the river of His power, which is the ever-flowing river of the Holy Spirit. As Christians, the Holy Spirit dwells in us. Nevertheless, it is imperative that we continue to draw from the Holy Spirit's strength and presence. We must stay in the word of God and pray without ceasing.

THE DEVOTED SERVANT

The devoted servant is one who says "yes" to the will of God—not out of compulsion, but out of love and willingness. The devoted servant gives his or her life to Jesus and does not take it back from Him. As a devoted servant of God, I see myself as a pitcher full of His power and abilities, and constantly pour myself out into the lives of others as I help them each day. Life is more than just "making it"; life is about making a difference. The apostle Paul said in Philippians 2:17 (NIV): "But even if I am being poured out like a drink offering on the sacrifice and service coming from your faith, I am glad and rejoice with all of you."

Paul was in prison when he penned these words. Yet he was pouring himself out to meet the needs of the people. A drink offering was poured out on the sacrifice in the morning and evening to demonstrate thanksgiving and faith. Paul was a true servant of Jesus Christ as he faced martyrdom.

Here's a definition of the word "servant," which comes from the Hebrew word *ebed* and the Greek word *diakonos:*

- One who is a slave or bondservant
- One who submits to the Master
- One who ministers
- One who meets the needs of others

D.L. Moody once said, "The measure of a man is not how many servants he has, but how many men he serves." True worth is measured by serving others or by meeting the needs of other people. People don't care how much we know until they know how much we care. Jesus is pleased when we care for the less fortunate.

In John 12:26 (KJV), Jesus says: "If any man serve Me, let him follow Me; and where I am, there shall also My servant be: if any man serve Me, him will My Father honour."

We serve other people by meeting their needs and by helping them in areas of desperation. People who are poor, needy, and destitute are referred to by Jesus as the "least of these." We serve Jesus by meeting the needs of the least of these (Matthew 25:40). We were not called to stay in our comfort zones—we were called to let our light shine and illuminate a dark and hurting world.

There is a story about a lady who worked in an office for a major corporation. When she started that job, she placed a flashlight in her desk drawer, in case the lights went out. About two years later, she was cleaning her desk drawer and discovered the flashlight. When she tried to take the batteries out, she discovered that battery acid had corroded the entire inside of the flashlight. She thought to herself, these batteries were new when I put them inside the flashlight. Now, they are no good. The moral of this story is that the lady had stored the flashlight in a warm, safe place with the batteries inside. But batteries were not made to be warm and comfortable. They were made to be put to use. We are like those flashlight batteries. We were not made to shut ourselves away in our comfort zones, or to be warm and comfortable. We were made to be put to use; we were made to let our light shine and make a difference in the world.

Jesus says in Matthew 20:26–28 (NIV): "Whoever wants to become great among you must be your servant, and whoever wants to be first must be your slave. Just as the Son of Man did not come to be served, but to serve, and to give His life as a ransom for many."

Jesus' mission for coming into the world was to die for our sins—to give His life for payment or ransom for our sins. He served mankind by shedding His blood on the cross. He did not demand that we serve Him or try to repay Him for His act of love. There is nothing that we can do to repay Jesus for all that He has done for us. The best thing we can do is to be a devoted servant. Jesus said that the greatest among us will be our servant (Matthew 23:11). This means that Jesus views greatness by the service that one renders. People who give of themselves to serve others are special in the eyes of Jesus.

Devotion to God means having a heart that is after God's own heart. This is the testimony that God gave concerning David. God said that David was a man after His own heart, who would do everything He wanted him to do (Acts 13:22). Wouldn't it be commendable if God were to give that same testimony concerning each one of us? We can all attest to the fact that David was far from perfect, yet God commends him with great esteem.

Being a man or woman after God's own heart has nothing to do with whether or not we have committed great sins. Receiving such a testimony from God comes when we seek after God with our whole heart. The key word here is "after." "After" is a preposition that means "in search of" or "in pursuit of." We must desire God to such a degree that we are constantly searching for Him. We must hunger and thirst for Him. The Bible says in Psalm 34:8 (KJV), "O taste and see that the Lord is good: blessed is the man that trusteth in Him."

David tasted of the goodness of God through personal experience. The word "taste" means to experience the flavor of something. We can only experience the flavor of God by getting to know Him and forming a genuine relationship with Him. God is not hiding from us. To seek God in relationship means we must desire to do His will, and we must strive to please Him by getting to know Him. God, in Jeremiah 29:13–14a (NIV), says, "You will seek Me and find Me when you seek Me with all your heart. I will be found by you."

Seeking the Lord means we are seeking His presence. The word "presence" in Hebrew means "face." When we seek God's presence, we are seeking His face. God is not far from those who seek Him with their whole heart. We will not seek God if we don't first desire Him. David says in Psalm 40:8 (KJV), "I delight to do thy will, O my God: Yea, Thy law is within my heart."

God's word must be nestled in our hearts so that we can meditate on Him and make a deliberate effort to obey

Him. With such busy schedules today, many people don't make time to read and study God's Word. The operative phrase is "make time." Many people fail to make time for the things of God. Real love and real relationships necessitate the giving of one's time. As a shepherd boy, David spent much time with God. He was constantly in the open field tending his sheep. God demonstrated His protection, His provision, His power, and His promises to David. From this experience, David was able to write the Twenty-third Psalm, depicting his relationship with God as Shepherd.

Since David knew God as Shepherd, he had no problem slaying Goliath, the nine-foot-tall giant. David told King Saul and the others around him, "The Lord who delivered me from the paw of the lion and the paw of the bear will deliver me from the hand of this Philistine" (I Samuel 17:37 NIV).

David was confident because God had delivered him from the lion and bear while tending his sheep. Whatever God has done for us in the past, He will do again. His love never fails. David continued to attest to God's faithfulness as he talked to Goliath and the spectators. He said in I Samuel 17:47 (NIV), "All those gathered here will know that it is not by sword or spear that the Lord saves; for the battle is the Lord's, and He will give all of you into our hands."

What are your Goliaths today? In other words, what giants do you face? Just remember that the battle is not yours; it is the Lord's. God has promised to fight our battles. As Christians we face each battle or challenge in the name of the Lord Almighty—the God of the armies of Israel. We must keep the faith that God will never leave us nor forsake us. He is always with us as our shepherd and we have everything that we need (Psalm 23:1).

I know that many of us wonder about the fact that David committed heinous sins against God, even as God said that he was a man after God's own heart. Here is the notable trait about David: He repented with a sincere heart. When David committed adultery with Bathsheba and had her husband Uriah killed by placing him on the front line of battle, the prophet Nathan came to him and confronted him about his sin. David realized that he had sinned against God. He said the following to Nathan in II Samuel 12:13–14 (NIV): "I have sinned against the Lord." Nathan replied, "The Lord has taken away your sin. You are not going to die. But because by doing this you have made the enemies of the Lord show utter contempt, the son born to you will die."

David knew his sins were serious, and he thought that he was going to die. Although he did not die, he had to face the consequences. The baby born out of that adulterous relationship died. David mourned heavily over this death. Because of David's sins, David's enemies displayed great disrespect for God. Many times we fail to realize that our sins affect those around us. The world will disrespect God because of our sinful behavior. Sure, God will forgive us our sins, but we will have to face the consequences, and potentially cause unbelievers to show utter contempt or disrespect for God.

Whenever we sin, we must repent. "Repent" means to turn from sin and turn to God; to have a change of mind and heart. David repented openly. In Psalm 51:1–2 (KJV), he prayed: "Have mercy upon me, O God, according to Thy loving kindness: according unto the multitude of Thy tender mercies blot out my transgressions. Wash me thoroughly from mine iniquity, and cleanse me from my sin."

In this prayer, David prayed that God would "un-sin" him. In essence, this is what repentance does. When we confess our sins before God, He is faithful and just, and He will forgive us our sins and cleanse us from all unrighteousness (I John 1:9).

God wants us as Christians to live a devoted life—a life that is separated unto Him. "Separated unto God" means that we are holy or set apart for God's service. In order to be fully devoted followers of Jesus Christ, we must invite Jesus into our heart. If you want to become a Christian by inviting Jesus into your heart, just pray the following prayer:

THE SINNER'S PRAYER

Lord, Jesus, I am a sinner.

Please forgive me of all my sins and cleanse me from all unrighteousness.

I believe that You died for me on the cross and that You rose again.

Come now, Lord Jesus, and live Your life in me.

Fill me, Lord, with Your Holy Spirit.

Thank You, Lord, for saving me.

In Jesus' name I pray. Amen.

If you prayed this prayer for the first time, you are now born again. You need to be baptized and live a devoted life for Jesus.

CHAPTER EIGHT

WINNING THROUGH FREEDOM IN JESUS

So if the Son sets you free, you will be free indeed.

JOHN 8:36 (NIV)

We are running this Christian race to win it. It's imperative to realize that we have been freed from the chains of sin and bondage so that we can run this race in victory. God's word says in Galatians 5:1 (NIV): "It is for freedom that Christ has set us free. Stand firm, then, and do not let yourselves be burdened again by a yoke of slavery."

Since Jesus has already paid our sin debt on the cross, let's not return to a life of sin. We have already been set free. To tamper with sin is to invite Satan's control back into our lives. I read a quote once that said, "If you play on the devil's playground, you will bring home his toys." This means that we should not hang around with the wrong crowd or listen to music that is inappropriate because the negative influence will remain in our spirit. We might think that a little bit of sinful behavior is innocent, but the results are detrimental. Sin takes us farther than we want to go; we stay longer than we want to stay; and we pay more than we want to pay. Jesus has already set us free; let's stand firm and remain faithful to Jesus.

Here's a definition of the word "freedom":

- Condition of *not* being bound, imprisoned, or enslaved
- Absence of constraints
- The state of being delivered

Romans 6:14 and 18 (NIV) says: "For sin shall not be your master, because you are not under law, but under grace. You have been set free from sin and have become slaves to righteousness."

Grace means unmerited favor and enablement from God to do what He has called us to do. Since we are under grace, we are slaves to righteousness. We are naturally bound by righteousness because we have the nature of Christ. We have been clothed in His righteousness.

Remember, it is for freedom that Christ has set us free. No one wants to be bound or enslaved to someone else's control. I once observed a rabbit struggling tenaciously to free itself from a defective chain-link fence. The wire from the fence had pinned the rabbit while it was trying to exit our yard. Every jerk and turn was to no avail. Out of fear, the rabbit managed to launch forward while tearing a gaping hole in its flesh. Although the rabbit leaped away injured, it was free. The damage to the rabbit was worth the price of freedom. The freedom we achieved from Jesus's death was greater than the pain He endured. Love nailed Jesus to the cross, and He would have died if you were the only person on earth. Nevertheless, he died to save the entire world from sin and destruction.

Jesus paid the price for our freedom. He went to Calvary and bled and died so that we could walk in total deliverance. Jesus is our release from bondage. All of us were bound by sin, and were unable to free ourselves. Satan had us trapped in his snare. Nevertheless, Jesus set us free. Isaiah 53:5 (KJV) says: "But He was wounded for our transgressions, He was bruised for our iniquities: the chastisement of our peace was upon Him; and with His stripes we are healed."

When Jesus brought us healing through the cross, He healed us in every fiber of our being. This healing included our emotions and sense of worth. There was a time in my life when my thoughts about myself were in bondage. My feeling of self-worth was at an all-time low. In other words, I was chained in the mind. One of the worst kinds of bondage is to be mentally enslaved. Proverbs 23:7 (NKJV) says: "For as he thinks in his heart, so is he."

So, what did I think of myself? Deep down inside, I felt like I was inferior to others, and I felt as though I could not do things as well as others. My parents showered a lot of love upon all of their children. There was no doubt in my mind that they loved me. The problem was how I felt inside, due to a society that insisted that I was inferior. Coming from a family where there was a great deal of poverty communicated to me that I was inferior. God began to speak to me, letting me know that He did not create me as an inferior. I began to realize that I could achieve whatever I believed inside. The greatest lesson I learned was that we are not defined by our circumstances. We might come from impoverished backgrounds, but our possibilities are not impoverished. God has wonderful plans for all of His children.

The Bible says in Ephesians 2:10 (NIV): "For we are

God's workmanship, created in Christ Jesus to do good works, which God prepared in advance for us to do."

We are a masterpiece that God thought of before the foundation of the world. Anything that is created is created twice—once in the mind and once in actuality. God thought of us before we even came into existence. Just that thought alone should motivate us concerning God's great love for us. Ephesians 3:20–21 (NKJV) says: "Now to Him who is able to do exceedingly abundantly above all that we ask or think, according to the power that works in us, to Him be glory in the church by Christ Jesus to all generations, forever and ever. Amen."

Creating us as his masterpiece, God placed the power of His Holy Spirit inside us, enabling us to accomplish all that we were created to do. Satan wants to limit us by making us believe that we cannot achieve, and that we are inferior in design. We must guard against Satan's mental schemes to destroy our sense of purpose. We can be bound mentally and not even know it. Sometimes we can accept our status in life without attempting to rise above the circumstances. We convince ourselves that our plight is what God intended for us. Therefore, we become unconsciously bound.

I read a story about a dog that was bound and became unconscious of it because it had fallen asleep. The owner of the dog had forgotten that he had chained the dog in the back yard and yelled, "Here, boy. Come here, boy." The dog plunged forward and didn't realize that it was bound. The pull of the chain jerked the dog back in place. The dog did not realize that it was chained until it tried to get free. Bondage of any kind is the same way. We can be mentally bound and not even realize it until we try to rise to a higher level. God wants us to be free in all areas of our lives, so we can ascend to the heights that He intended.

THREE WAYS TO BE ALL THAT GOD INTENDED

1. Know who you are.

As Christians, we are children of God. Everybody was created by God, but not everybody is a child of God. Once we become born again, we are God's children. Romans 8:15–17 (NIV) says: "For you did not receive a spirit that makes you a slave again to fear, but you received the Spirit of sonship. And by Him we cry, 'Abba, Father.' The Spirit Himself testifies with our spirit that we are God's children. Now if we are children, then we are heirs—heirs of God and co-heirs with Christ, if indeed we share in His sufferings in order that we may also share in His glory."

"Abba, Father" means that we have a personal relationship with God the Father. He is like our "daddy" or "papa." We can disclose our deepest thoughts and needs to Him. We are God's children by adoption through grace. As adopted children, we have all the rights of the natural son, including inheritance rights. Jesus is God's son by nature; we are God's children by grace. The Holy Spirit inside of us is God's seed unfolding inside of us to make us like Him. We have God's DNA—therefore, we should look like Him and act like Him.

Since we have inheritance rights, one day we will go to heaven to receive our glorified bodies where we will be able to be exactly like Jesus in all of His glory. While we are on earth, suffering helps us to conform to the image of Christ Jesus. We will be totally like Him in heaven.

As God's child, I can say, "The Lord is my Shepherd, I shall not want" (Psalm 23:1, KJV). This means that God cares for me and tends to me as His sheep. God will supply everything I need because He cares for me as His child.

2. Know how you are created.

As God's children, we are uniquely created. Psalm 139:13–14 (NIV) says: "For you created my inmost being; you knit me together in my mother's womb. I praise you because I am fearfully and wonderfully made; Your works are wonderful, I know that full well."

The word "fearfully" means awesome, and the word "wonderfully" means excellent. This means that we are awesome and excellent. Such a description should make all of us feel special and empowered. God did not create us as misfits, or by accident. We are created with such precision and uniqueness that no one else has our fingerprints or DNA. We are wonderful and excellent because God is wonderful and excellent. We are created like God. Genesis 1:27 (KJV) says: "So God created man in His own image, in the image of God created He him; male and female created He them."

Just like God, we are holy, righteous, worthy of honor, and made to rule over creation. God has favored us with a special place in His creation. Just like our earthly parents, God wants us to represent Him well. Many times when our boys—Charlie Jr. and Andrew—were growing up, I would say, "Boys, you better not embarrass me." This meant that I wanted them to behave in a manner that reflected my teaching and training. People see the impact we have made on our children. Our DNA is flowing through their systems; our name is stamped on their character. Likewise, God wants us to represent Him well. When people see us, they should say, "There goes a child of God; they look just like the Heavenly Father."

3. Know why you are created.

Do you know your purpose for being on this earth? In

every season of my life, I discover that God unfolds His good and perfect plans for me. Out of every trial, God conforms me to His image, and He uses each trial to equip me for the next phase of His purpose for me. God has good things in store for all of His children. Jeremiah 29:11 (KJV) says: "'For I know the thoughts that I think toward you,' saith the Lord. 'Thoughts of peace, and not of evil, to give you an expected end.'"

I was talking to a friend who is going through a difficult time, and he asked, "Why is God mad at me?" I told him that God was not mad at Him, and that God would use that situation to make Him stronger. I reassured him that God has wonderful plans for him, and that God was not trying to do him harm. Currently, I don't think he can see hope for the future because of the dark clouds over his head. By faith, he will gradually see that God is in control and knows what He is doing.

None of us is an accident. My being born for such a time as this completes God's design for what is occurring in the rest of the world. The world was not ready for me a hundred years ago. This is my time to shine for the glory of God. You and I have been groomed to impact the world in this phase of history. No one else can do our job for us. We have an eternal assignment to win souls in our own sphere of influence. Let's not let God down. Let's walk worthy of the calling that He has placed on our lives. With each step we take, God will unfold His direction and scheme for us. We must stay focused and keep the faith!

THE BONDAGE OF WORRY

Worry disconnects us from God. It is a profound form of unbelief and is manifested by fear. Corrie ten Boom (a

Dutch watchmaker who helped many Jews escape the Nazi Holocaust during World War II) said, "Worry does not empty tomorrow of sorrows; it empties today of strength." In other words, worry weighs us down!

Here's a definition of the word "worry":

- Mental uneasiness caused by fear
- Anxiety
- The enabling of one's mind to dwell on difficulty or trouble

Worry is a condition of the mind where the enemy does battle. The more we worry, the more inundated we become with it. It propels us into a state of bondage. Before we know it, we are overwhelmed with so much distress that we require medical attention. The Bible says in Philippians 4:6 (KJV): "Be careful for nothing; but in everything by prayer and supplication with thanksgiving let your requests be made known unto God."

This verse tells us not to worry or not to become anxious. Worry and anxiety are the opposite of faith. Remember, faith pleases God. God wants us to pray about everything and worry about nothing. Rather than worrying, we need to present our requests to God with thanksgiving in our hearts.

Jesus tells us in Matthew 6:31–34 (NIV): "So do not worry, saying, 'What shall we eat?' or 'What shall we drink?' or 'What shall we wear?' For the pagans run after all these things, and your heavenly Father knows that you need them. But seek first his Kingdom and His righteousness, and all these things will be given to you as well. Therefore do not worry about tomorrow, for tomorrow will worry about itself. Each day has enough trouble of its own."

When we worry, we take God off the throne and put

ourselves on the throne of our lives. Kingdom living is predicated on the fact that God is sovereign and He is the ultimate ruler. If we make Him first, worry will vanish. God wants us to put Him first; it shows that we have our priorities in order.

THREE THINGS THAT WORRY CAN DO

1. Worry can dominate us.

In Luke 10:38–39 (NIV), we see that Martha was overtaken by worry. She opened her home to Jesus and there were so many preparations to make. The passage reads as follows: "As Jesus and His disciple were on their way, He came to a village where a woman named Martha opened her home to Him. She had a sister called Mary, who sat at the Lord's feet listening to what He said."

Are you a "Martha" or a "Mary"? Do you get easily overwhelmed and stressed out over all that you have to do in a given day? Or do you give your cares to Jesus and seek Him first? Jesus is not telling us not to take responsibility and not to do our fair share of work—He is telling us to not put that work before him. Martha operated in a strong gift of hospitality, which was expected in Biblical customs. However, we should never put more emphasis on the gift than on its giver.

2. Worry can distract us.

The word "distract" means to divert the mind. Worry causes us to lose focus. Luke 10:40 (NIV) says: "But Martha was distracted by all the preparations that had to be made. She came to Him and asked, 'Lord, don't you care that my sister has left me to do the work by myself? Tell her to help me!'"

Martha was frustrated and really hoped that Jesus would force her younger sister, Mary, to help her. Both Martha and Mary loved Jesus. Nevertheless, Martha was devoid of devotion to our Lord. Mary is constantly at the Savior's feet. I think about us as Christians. When we invite Jesus into our heart, we are inviting Him into our home. Once He is inside, how do we treat Him? Do we ignore him because of how busy we are? Or do we long to sit at His feet? In Psalm 27:4 (NIV), David says: "One thing I ask of the Lord, this is what I seek: that I may dwell in the house of the Lord all the days of my life, to gaze upon the beauty of the Lord and to seek Him in His temple."

It is extremely refreshing to dwell in the presence of the Lord. There was a lady in our church who had a massive tumor removed from her uterus. The night before the surgery, she was overcome with worry. She said that she cried like a baby for several minutes. Then all of a sudden, she cast those cares upon Jesus, and she immediately entered into His presence. While in His presence, she achieved perfect peace. The surgery was a total success and she had a rapid recovery with no complications. God touched her body in a miraculous way, because she turned from worry to faith.

3. Worry can deceive us.

We can be deceived by worry, thinking that things will improve if we worry about them. I heard a person say once that worry is like a rocking chair; it gives you something to do, but it doesn't get you anywhere.

In Luke 10:41 (NIV), Jesus says: "Martha, Martha, you are worried and upset about many things."

This passage indicates that we can be worried and upset at the same time. Martha was worried because she had the responsibility of making all of the necessary preparations for Jesus and His disciples, since His disciples were traveling with Him. She was upset because Mary was not helping her. I can sense that Martha was overwhelmed! Jesus had a response for her in Luke 10:42 (NIV). He says: "But only one thing is needed. Mary has chosen what is better, and it will not be taken away from her."

Seeking the Kingdom first is a choice. Mary chose Jesus above all else. Despite the magnitude of our circumstances, we must always choose Jesus. This requires sitting down internally and spending time with our Master.

God tells us in Psalm 46:10 (KJV), "Be still, and know that I am God: I will be exalted among the heathen, I will be exalted in the earth." This Scripture is the key to true devotion. It gives us the key to how to enter God's presence and find His peace.

SAVED FROM SIN'S SHACKLES

Whatever our sin may be, whether it is worry or gossip, we can be rescued from its grip. Sin shackles us, which means that it fastens us or confines us by its weight. A mother was talking to her daughter about the effects of sin. The mother quoted the famous statement about the devil's playground. She said, "If we play on the devil's playground, we will bring home his toys."

After pondering these words, the little girl replied, "If I played on the devil's playground, he'd eat my lunch."

Children make such profound statements. The truth of the matter is that the devil has come to take our lunch. He has come to take our joy, our mind, our happiness, and our testimony. Jesus tells us in John 10:10 (NIV), "The thief comes only to steal and kill and destroy; I have come that they may have life, and have it to the full."

Jesus taught us much about Satan's evil plans and destructive schemes. Nevertheless, Jesus has a counter-plan to give us eternal life in heaven and abundant life right here on this earth. In order to achieve this tremendous blessing, we must make Jesus the Lord of our lives and make the choice to repent of our sins. Sin has weight, and Hebrews 12:1 (NIV) says: "Therefore, since we are surrounded by such a great cloud of witnesses, let us throw off everything that hinders, and the sin that so easily entangles. And let us run with perseverance the race marked out for us."

Deciding to abandon the sin that is entangling us is a choice that we as Christians must make in order to be free of Satan's control. The great cloud of witnesses mentioned in the verse above refers to the heroes of faith who have gone on to heaven before us. We have the entire heavenly host cheering us on to victory, just like in an athletic event with many people in the stadium. We are engaged in a race, and we must continue to run tenaciously in order to achieve our goal—which is our heavenly reward. It takes determination and perseverance to run this race. Just like in any race, we must remain focused on the finish line; for us, Jesus is our finish line! He is the author and finisher of our faith (Hebrews 12:2).

The Word of God is powerful—so powerful that we can hide it in our heart. Psalm 119:11 (KJV) says: "Thy Word have I hid in mine heart, that I might not sin against Thee."

God's Word must be hidden in our hearts for safekeeping. That Word will grow within us and reap a harvest. The Word of God inside us will mature into effective battle gear against Satan. The only Word that is going to change us is the Word that is inside us; that Word makes us mighty in battle. The Word inside us will become a sword that we can use to aggressively fight the enemy. All that we need to run this race is inside us. Jesus is the Word inside us, enabling us to overcome the shackles of sin's power. Remember, "If the Son therefore shall make you free, ye shall be free indeed" (John 8:36, KJV).

BECOME A CHRISTIAN

If you want to invite Jesus into your heart so that you can be free from the shackles of sin, just pray the following prayer: Once you have prayed this prayer, you should contact your pastor or some other spiritual leader.

THE SINNER'S PRAYER

Lord, Jesus, I am a sinner.

Please forgive me of all my sins and cleanse me from all unrighteousness.

I believe that You died for me on the cross and that You rose again.

Come now, Lord Jesus, and live Your life in me.

Fill me, Lord, with Your Holy Spirit.

Thank You, Lord, for saving me.

In Jesus' name I pray. Amen.

If you prayed this prayer for the first time, you are now born again. You are now a Christian. You need to be baptized and live a victorious life for Jesus! Remember, you are in this Christian race to win it—and you can win in every round or season of your life!

BIBLIOGRAPHY

The Holy Bible, Containing the Old and New Testaments, New King James Version: Nashville: Thomas Nelson Bibles, 1994.

The Holy Bible: English Standard Version, Containing the Old and New Testaments. Wheaton: Crossway, 2001.

Holy Bible TBN Parallel Edition King James Version and New Living Translation (TBN Special Edition). Carol Stream: Tyndale House Publishers, 2005.

The New International Webster's Pocket Dictionary of the English Language, New Revised Edition. Naples: Trident Press International, 2002.

NIV Study Bible: New International Version, Tenth Anniversary Edition. Grand Rapids: Zondervan Publishing House, 1995.

The Transformation Study Bible: New Living Translation. Colorado Springs: David C. Cook, 2009.

Vine, W.E. *Vine's Concise Dictionary of Bible Words.* Nashville: Thomas Nelson Publishers, 1999.

Webster's New Compact Dictionary for School and Office, Revised Edition. Nashville: Thomas Nelson Publishers, 1991.

Webster's New World Basic Dictionary of American English. Cleveland: Wiley Publishing, Inc., 1998.

The World Book Dictionary, Volume One (A–K). Chicago: Field Enterprises Educational Corporation, 1974.

The World Book Dictionary, Volume Two (L–Z). Chicago: Field Enterprises Educational Corporation, 1974.

MEET THE AUTHOR

PASTOR EARNESTINE BLAKLEY is a native of Steele, Missouri—located in the Missouri Bootheel. She currently resides in St. Joseph, Missouri, with her husband, Charles. They have two adult sons—Charles, Jr., and Andrew.

Pastor Blakley is the Pastor and Founder of Hope Fellowship Church in St. Joseph, Missouri. With the help and support of her husband, Charles, she founded this non-denominational ministry on June 4, 2009. The mission is to proclaim the Gospel of Jesus Christ so that others may know Him and make Him known through evangelism, worship, and discipleship.

Pastor Earnestine is also the founder and president of H.O.P.E. Outreach Ministries, Inc.—founded on June 13, 1994. (H.O.P.E. is an acronym for Helping Other People Excel.) The mission of this outreach ministry is to help the hurting and the needy find hope and spiritual nourishment through God's Word. Pastor Blakley and numerous volunteers read storybooks to children at apartment complexes during the summer months. During the school year, she arranges for students from local schools to visit the elderly in nursing homes so they can interact through games and conversation. Some of the objectives are to promote literacy, build relationships, foster volunteerism, and break down generational, socio-economic, cultural, and denominational barriers.

Pastor Blakley taught in the St. Joseph School District for fourteen years. During the 1991–92 school year, she was named St. Joseph Teacher of the Year and Missouri State Teacher of the Year. She has served on the National Education Panel for Energizer Battery, the State Committee for America 2000, the State Commission on Performance, and the National Writing Team for the Environmental Protection Agency. On April 20, 2011, she received the Roy Blunt Literacy Citation; on April 18, 2012, she received the Missouri Humanities Exemplary Community Achievement Award for Youth Literacy from the Missouri Humanities Council, in Jefferson City, Missouri.

During her teaching career, Pastor Blakley was named

"Woman of Distinction" for the Midland Empire Girl Scout Council; she has been listed in the *World's Who's Who of Women*, and the *Who's Who in American Education*. She was nominated for the Walt Disney American Teacher Awards, and was a national finalist for Project Self-Esteem.

Pastor Blakley has a weekly ministry on KQ2-TV, every Sunday morning at 9:00 a.m.; and a weekly radio ministry on KSJI Radio (91.1 FM), every Sunday morning at 9:30 a.m. In foreign ministry, Pastor Earnestine has preached and ministered in Guatemala, Venezuela, and the Bahamas.

Pastor Blakley has a Bachelor of Science Degree in Elementary Education from Lincoln University (in Jefferson City, Missouri); a Master of Science Degree in Education from Northwest Missouri State University (in Maryville, Missouri); an Honorary Doctorate of Humane Letters Degree from Maryville University (in St. Louis, Missouri); credentialing as an ordained minister from Global University of the Assemblies of God (in Springfield, Missouri); and a Writing Diploma from the Institute of Children's Literature (in Redding Ridge, Connecticut).

Pastor Earnestine Blakley is also the author of *Building Godly Habits*, published in 2015 by Inkwater Press.

CPSIA information can be obtained
at www.ICGtesting.com
Printed in the USA
FFHW02n1330050918
48141249-51861FF

9 781629 014524